GOD
IN THE
DARK
Through Grief and Beyond

Luci Shaw

ZondervanPublishingHouse
Grand Rapids, Michigan

A Division of HarperCollins*Publishers*

GOD IN THE DARK
Copyright © 1989 by Luci Shaw

First softcover edition 1993

Requests for information should be addressed to:
Zondervan Publishing House
Grand Rapids, Michigan 49530

Library of Congress Cataloging-in-Publication Data

Shaw, Luci.
    God in the dark / by Luci Shaw. – 1st ed.
      p. cm.
    "Broadmoor books."
    ISBN 0-310-20891-2
    1. Shaw, Luci. 2. Lungs—Cancer—Patients—United States—Family
relationships. 3. Wives—United States—Biography. 4. Christian
life—1960- I. Title.
    RC280.L8S52   1989
    362.1'9699424'0092–dc20   89-31975
    [B]   CIP

Poems from *Polishing the Petoskey Stone,* copyright © 1990 by Luci Shaw.
Used by permission of Harold Shaw Publishers. All other original poems
copyright © 1989 by Luci Shaw. Used by permission.

Printed in the United States of America

93 94 95 96 97 / CH / 10 9 8 7 6 5 4 3 2

GOD
IN THE
DARK

*This book is dedicated to the family of God
at St. Mark's Episcopal Church, Geneva, Illinois*

*. . . Now God comes to thee, as the sun at noon
to illustrate all shadowes, as the sheaves at harvest
to fill all penuries. . . . All occasions
invite his mercies, and all times are his seasons.*
John Donne, **Sermons**

CONTENTS

ACKNOWLEDGMENTS

I thank with all my heart not only the people who have lived with me through doubt and faith, darkness and light, despair and delight, but those who encouraged me to put in a book the thoughts I recorded in journals during a crucial thirty-six months of my life.

I thank each of my children, Robin, Marian, John, Jeffrey, and Kristin, for the warmth of their love and support. They have all read this book in its early drafts and have agreed to let me tell parts of their stories as well as my own.

I thank Richard Foster and the Friends University Faculty and Administration for their warm invitation to come to Wichita in the Fall of 1987 as a Visiting Fellow at the Milton Center in order to write this book. My gratitude goes to the Thursday critique group of Associate Fellows at the Center for bearing with me as I read large chunks of my early manuscript aloud to them. Their comments and criticisms were helpful and I took them seriously. I am particularly grateful to Harold Fickett for his penetrating, detailed, and unfailingly honest reading of the whole manuscript, his continued interest in its progress, and his encouragement of its author.

In a special critique group certain members of the Chrysostom Society—Philip Yancey, Walter Wangerin, Steve Law-head, Karen Mains, and myself—met to read portions of our ongoing manuscripts. Once again, I acknowledge their perceptive critical judgment and that of Shirley Nelson who read and critiqued the entire manuscript in its final form.

This book has been read and checked by some of the physicians mentioned in the narrative. My deep gratitude goes to them not only for their friendship and care during my husband's illness but for their attention to the medical procedures and details I have described. At their request I have changed some of their names and the names of the institutions they represent.

To my therapist, whose real name does not appear, my thanks for helping me to see myself and God more truly.

Finally, to Judith Markham for her confidence that I could write a prose book, to Bob Hudson for his guidance in revision, and to Anne Severance—my editor, who helped me tame a 900-page monster into a manageable book with sensitivity and skill—my special appreciation.

I

THE PESTILENCE THAT STALKS THE DARK

June–December 1984

Faustus: *Who made thee?*
Mephistopheles: *God; as the light makes*
  the shadow.
Faustus: *Is God, then, evil?*
Mephistopheles: *God is only light,*
  And in the heart of the light no shadow
    standeth,
  Nor can I dwell within the light of
    heaven
  Where God is all.
Faustus: *What art thou, Mephistopheles?*
Mephistopheles: *I am the price that all*
    things pay for being,
  The shadow on the world, thrown by
    the world
  Standing in its own light, which light
    God is.

  —DOROTHY SAYERS, **The Devil to Pay**

One

I remember. I remember the dark clouds moving across the years of my life, stretched like a field of prairie wheat in the sun, dulled by the sudden shadows. Like the wandering weather, my seasons of doubt and questioning have often come and then moved on.

Near the beginning of one of my longest, darkest cycles I remember praying with my friend Karen: "God, show me your self, your reality clear as the sun, no matter what it takes."

I didn't know what it would take.

Another prayer, later, under the same dark clouds: "Lord, I promise never to give up on you, never to desert the faith." Like a marriage vow that sometimes staples a faltering relationship, that promise held me during seven years in which I battled to know my God real in the dark while living in his silence, in the sense of his absence. Now and then lightning forked from the sky, like a mystical sword, or a watery sun gleamed from the earth's edge. Sometimes I felt a glimmering of spirit like a clear night in the country, away from the artificial city brightness, the whole sweep of sky like a star map, with the constellations not just pricks of light but three-dimensional—near stars, and far, the moon tracking her luminous voyage among them before dying below the horizon. But mostly it was a long darkness, like a sentence of death.

✻ One blazing hot day in June, my husband Harold, on a late-afternoon impulse, started up the power mower and cleared the overgrown lot behind our publishing building and warehouse in Wheaton, Illinois. Afterwards, covered with perspiration and grimy with dust, he came inside to the coolness of our air-conditioned offices. Most of our staff had gone home. As was often the case, we two were working late.

Suddenly I heard from his office an explosive sneeze, and a moment later a peculiarly urgent call, "Lu, come here. Quickly!"

As I came through his office door he was staring in amazement at the handkerchief in his hand. On it was a huge blood clot about the size of a plum. "When I sneezed, this came up into my throat and I spat it out," he explained. "What do you make of it?"

Shaken by the ominous look of the thing, I replied, "I don't know. But we'd better call Dr. Parker right away."

Paul Parker, Harold's long-time personal physician and close friend, asked us to meet him at the Emergency Room of our local hospital where he examined Harold and scheduled an x-ray.

"I think it's just from a bleeder," he told my husband. "Probably all the dust and chaff kicked up by the mower irritated your lungs and caused a minor hemorrhage. But let's do the x-ray to make sure."

When the film came back, it showed nothing abnormal. We breathed a double sigh of relief and almost forgot the whole incident in the next weeks of hectic preparation for the Christian Booksellers Association convention, to be held in July in Anaheim, California. CBA is an annual trade show where book publishers like us exhibit new books and take orders from the thousands of Christian bookstore buyers who attend. It is a week-long event, both emotionally exhilarating and physically exhausting.

I was scheduled to teach an intensive, three-week poetry workshop at Regent College in Vancouver. Two days after the end of the CBA convention, during the last week of July, 1984, Kristin, our youngest daughter, then fifteen years old, went with me to the Northwest to spend some time before the workshop with our oldest daughter, Robin, and her husband, Mark Schramer. The Schramers were renting a small farm-house in Washington's Whatcom County where Mark was starting his own construction business.

This left Harold at home alone in West Chicago for a three-week stretch. I had called some of our Wheaton friends and asked them to have him over for a good, home-cooked meal now and then. Otherwise, my sixty-seven-year-old husband would have to fend for himself, which he didn't mind doing, he said. Still the idea made me a little uneasy.

Once in Vancouver, I struggled to keep ahead of my twenty-five graduate-level students—studying and teaching in the mornings, spending long afternoon hours in my office for tutorials, and also preparing for several public lectures and a poetry reading.

One morning before class I had a disturbing long-distance call. It was from Harold. "I've had the flu," he told me, "and after days of wheezing and feeling weak and miserable, I finally went to Dr. Parker. He said it's walking pneumonia, and gave me some antibiotics. But he told me I need to stay in bed and rest."

I felt a wave of anxiety. "I should fly right home and take care of you. How are you going to rest when you have to get up to cook?"

Harold seemed amused by my concern. He sounded slightly

hoarse, but as we talked on the phone I could almost feel his strong, physical presence and see his square face lit with humor. "Don't worry, honey. I'm not too proud to ask someone to bring me food if I need it." He knew how hard it would be for me to leave in the middle of the course. Most of my students were taking it for credit and some had come from overseas. I felt torn by my urgent desire to be with Harold and my sense of commitment to Regent and the students.

"Let me think about it," I said after a short pause. "I love you." I hung up the phone, and walked to chapel. I was late. As I mounted the steps to the back entrance, I heard the student body singing "Our God Reigns," and my heart grasped at the words, reminded that God saw me and Harold, that we were joined in his powerful mercy. I stayed at Regent, calling Harold every day as he recuperated, trying to pull things together for him from 2500 miles away.

At the conclusion of the course Kris and I flew home to West Chicago. By that time Harold seemed to be nearly recovered—still coughing a bit, and sometimes short of breath, but going in to the office every day during one of the busiest times of our publishing year.

✱ For several months we had planned a long weekend at the Shakespeare Festival in Stratford, Ontario with close friends—four other couples from St. Mark's Episcopal Church with whom we met regularly. The Group—David and Karen Mains, Jack Risley and Marlene LeFever, Eric and Pennie Thurman, Rick and Donna Lobs (our rector and his wife), and Harold and I—were all Christians, springing from differing evangelical backgrounds, and all of us longed to be on the cutting edge where faith and reality meet. Most of us were active in public ministries of various kinds, and we needed at the center of our lives others with whom we could find intimacy.

It was a magical weekend. The weather was crisp, our expectations high. We saw Molière as well as Shakespeare, visited bookshops and galleries and some great restaurants, and felt carefree, but not careless.

The final night, though, Harold had trouble breathing. He said he felt smothered, and couldn't sleep until he propped himself up in bed with pillows and opened all the windows. The following morning he stayed in bed in the guest house to rest while I went to the bank for cash. Eric took my arm as I was leaving the bank and said quietly, "I don't want to alarm you, but do you have any contingency plans in case something happens to Harold?" I looked at him rather blankly. Harold and I were generally healthy people from long-lived families and, yes, we had a will, but no, we hadn't thought much about "anything happening" to either of us.

Back in West Chicago, Harold had a few more coughing and wheezing episodes the next week, but the following Friday (in his inveterate do-it-yourself way), he insisted on cutting the acre of grass around our house, using our riding mower—a three-hour job. He seemed tired and choked up when he came in, and lay down, complaining of pressure in his chest. A pulled muscle, maybe?

In the night the pressure intensified and became severe pain. As he found breathing more and more difficult we began to panic. Was this a heart attack? Very early that Saturday morning, while it was still dark, I drove him to the Emergency Room of our local hospital, thankful that it was only ten minutes away.

I have always experienced a strange excitement in emergency rooms. With five curious children and their inevitable oral experimentation with pills, mothballs, Christmas balls (yes!), paint, and other ingestibles, I'd been in local ER's often enough. I don't know what it is that I find so gripping—perhaps seeing how people react to crisis, the challenge of remaining cool and calm myself, my love for medical settings and the fascination of medical technology, my affinity for the profession—after all, both my grandfathers, my father, brother, and son were or are physicians.

The ER doctor on duty checked Harold over, had him x-rayed, and gave him a shot. Slowly the pain began to subside and he could breathe more easily. The doctor observed him there for a few hours, then sent him home with me with more medication and instructions to rest. But Saturday evening the pain and pressure began to build again and once more we made the midnight trip to the hospital.

I remember how warm it was. Stars filled the night, and I felt the contrast between the constriction of Harold's breathing and the wide, deep, velvet freedom of the dark sky. Silently I asked, *God, are you out there?*

This time, when he was x-rayed, the film showed only a blank opacity in the area where his left lung should have been. "His lung has collapsed," said the ER physician, shaking his head, hanging the films up on the light panel and pointing out the difference between the film taken the previous night and the one they had just developed. The medical report called it "opacification of the left hemithorax." The diagnosis was "complete atelectasis." The lung collapse suggested a blockage in the air passage through the left bronchus. Swelling? Mucus? A tumor? All of a sudden this trip was no longer an adventure but a threat. While Harold was admitted as an inpatient, I filled out forms and answered questions.

I suddenly realized how I'd lost track of time. This was the morning of the Sunday school picnic at St. Mark's Episcopal Church. The morning Eucharist was to be held outside in someone's garden, and afterwards everyone would lunch there together.

I found a phone, called Kris at home, and our curate, Carl Brenner, explaining to him why we could not be there. He must have passed the news quickly because soon I saw Karen walking through the hospital entrance. She spent most of the morning with me, waiting for a bronchoscopy to be done. Though full of people, the hospital was a lonely place. Having my friend to stay and pray with me defused some of my growing anxiety and fatigue.

The next days are a blur in my mind—gleaming, endless hospital corridors, elevators, food trays, wheelchairs, flowers, phone calls, tests, and doctors in hospital greens, the jargon of their medical reports as cold and flat as the days we were living.

Harold was admitted to the hospital Intensive Care Unit on September 9, 1984.

His first bronchoscopy revealed "a red, smooth mass with the appearance of a bronchial adenoma." However, the biopsy showed only "fibrin with entrapped red cells and no evidence of inflammation or malignancy."

His cardiac workup was normal.

Because he continued to have pain and shortness of breath, he was advised to stay in hospital under observation in the hope that the obstruction would clear spontaneously.

During that first week Harold had blood taken for a CEA test. A blood factor known as Carcinogenic Embryonic Antigen sometimes indicates the presence of a lung, liver, or breast cancer. The normal reading is 2 or 3. When the results came back, Harold's CEA level was 16.6, the first sign that something ominous was going on. At this point his surgeon's report stated: "This most likely is a carcinoma."

But a second bronchoscopy September 17 was inconclusive. The biopsy obtained showed only cellular debris (from the bronchial wall) which "lacked structural integrity."

A liver scan on September 18 was "negative for metastatic disease."

Our son John, who had graduated from medical school the Spring before, arrived from Florida where he was doing his internship in the Navy. To have him with us, with a working knowledge of hospitals, medical technology, and terminology was a huge help. Tall, thin, blond, his sensitive face alive with humor, John, with his active Christian faith and sympathetic presence, was a strength to us that went way beyond mere information.

As test after test proved negative or inconclusive, we were suspended in unknowing.

Finally, on September 24, the surgeons decided to "go in and see what was going on." Excerpts from the surgeons' report tell the story:

> An incision was made and the chest was entered through the interspace. Examination demonstrated the hilum to be free of tumor, as was the liver. . . .
>
> The upper lobe had a small mass between the size of a walnut to a golf ball in it, and this had the feeling of a benign lesion. The mediastinum was opened in the aortic window. There were 2 or 3 one-half cm. soft lymph nodes noted which appeared to be slightly whiter and more watery than usual. These were removed and sent to the laboratory for frozen section, and in the meantime, with the feeling that this most likely represented a benign endobronchial process, the patient was prepared for a left upper lobe resection.
>
> When the frozen section came back from the lab it was reported as "*adenocarcinoma metastatic to nodes.*" Therefore it was felt best to proceed with a pneumonectomy (removal of lung), rather than a lobectomy. (In other words, the lymph node was cancerous and the whole lung, rather than one lobe, had to be removed.)

The report ends with the statement: "The family was notified of the findings."

It was at this point that I was called into the surgeon's office. Karen was with me. The surgeon said, quite unemotionally, as if discussing a problem with a car transmission, "Your husband has lung cancer. He has a life expectancy of less than eighteen months."

I asked if I could sit down.

With his words, clear and colorless, hanging in the air, I felt no sorrow or grief, just an awful numbness. I couldn't cry. I remember that in a terrible effort to move towards normalcy, like rising from a dive under water to the surface of a lake, I asked him some questions, though I can't recall them. My legs felt heavy, as if I'd been drugged.

While Karen went to call our rector, Rick Lobs, the doctor sketched some diagrams on a prescription pad to explain to John, Jeff (our younger son), and me the details of the surgery. Then there was nothing to do but go to the ICU waiting room and sit there in the plastic chairs until Harold could be moved to Recovery where we would see him.

Rick arrived—a man vigorous in body and spirit. He sat with us while I told him all I knew, and he prayed, his strong face alight with concern.

I kept having to explain the diagnosis to every new friend who came into the waiting room: "Harold has lung cancer. Yes, the lung was removed, but the surgeon says it's terminal," and felt the truth sinking deeper into me with each retelling. I had a sensation of running without motion, as in a nightmare.

Two

Lately (I recorded in my journal) I've dreamed of standing at a pond's edge and watching the edges of ice crystals shooting their spears across the motionless, fluid surface. And wanting my camera. And stumbling home for the camera, but never finding it. Dave Singer and I have talked about *experiencing* art or beauty versus *talking* about it. The moment you start to analyze, you step back out of the experience itself to an evaluation of it. You lose its immediacy. I ache to be joined to these moments of vision, but distance and time intervene, and I lose all but the fleet glimpse.

I want also to catch and preserve the pain of these days— learning about life with cancer. The hours won't linger to be experienced again, but they are valuable, precious. All I can hope is that these words in my journal (which was to record the details of our lives for the next thirty-six months) will summon up enough detail to recall some of each hour's immediate reality, so they will not be lost in a blur of forgetfulness.

❋ *September 25, 1984*—John left for Pensacola by plane yesterday morning. We woke at 5:00 A.M., picked up Jeff in Wheaton, and drove to the airport. It was so hard to see John leave. Parting is a tearing. His firm, intelligent support has been like a splint on a fractured leg.

Jeff was unshaven and exhausted and, after returning from the airport, I dropped him off at his apartment to get some more sleep. He has just resigned from his position with the Waldner Corporation and taken a job with Timber Hill Industries. When he finishes his training period, he will have a seat on the New York Stock Exchange. Harold's surgery and prognosis make this a difficult transition for him. The discovery of the cancer makes him question the wisdom of leaving for New York right now.

Since it was still early in the morning, I drove past Clyde and Martha Kilby's, on Jefferson Street. Clyde was throwing nuts to his squirrels from an upstairs window and I opened my car window and shouted, "Throw me a nut, too?" He called back, "Come up and have breakfast." It was good to be with these, our oldest, dearest friends in Wheaton. They wanted to know all about Harold. Clyde was my teacher when I was an English Lit major in the early fifties. He is still my mentor as well as "honorary grandfather" to all our children.

❋ Back at home, Kris told me the surgeon had called. His news: Harold had to be taken back to surgery. A blood clot had formed when a "pumper" opened up and bled about two pints' worth of blood into the lung. So again he had been cut open, the clot removed, the intercostal artery resutured, and the area around the incision cauterized. How invasive surgery is. We are learning the meaning of *trauma*.

On hearing this news I rushed over to the hospital. (I'm

grateful that the office, the hospital, and home are only ten minutes apart as I triangulate between them.) Harold had just been moved from the Recovery room to the Intensive Care Unit, and it took at least twenty minutes for the nurses to get all his tubes, dressings, IV bottles, and various monitors arranged and hooked up before I was allowed to see him.

He is full of morphine. Eyes closed. Skin pale and clammy. A respirator breathes for him, the air being pushed through a tube in his tracheostomy. But he is able to squeeze my hand when I slide it into his, and to turn his head toward my kiss. The hardest things for me to see are his pain in spite of the morphine, his immobility, his absolute dependence, his help-lessness, and his inability to communicate. We are so dreadfully cut off from our usual closeness. Harold has never been as verbal as I am, but this—this artificial silence seems unbear-able.

Next day we learn the physicians' preliminary diagnosis: "The left lung shows mucin-producing adenocarcinoma of the upper lobe, arising in the major bronchus, with metastasis to two of four peribronchial lymph nodes." The spread of the cancer is bad news.

I call to you, O Lord, every day;
I spread out my hands to you.
Do you show your wonders to the dead?
Do those who are dead rise up and praise you?
Is your love declared in the grave,
Your faithfulness in Destruction?
Are your wonders known in the place of darkness?

I have suffered your terrors and am in despair.
All day long they surround me like a flood;
You have taken my companion, my loved one
        from me . . .
Darkness is my intimate friend.
        —(Ps. 88:13, 10–12, 16–18)

The sort of unrelieved gloom that gripped David in this psalm is attacking me today. This morning's *Today Show* featured rates of cure for different kinds of cancer. Lung cancer has one of the lowest cure rates: 8–12 percent. More reality therapy. I am feeling an urgent need to be alone—to think everything through without "projecting," but without denying any of the facts.

* Yesterday Harold was more alert but in much pain. I was there when the doctor removed the drainage tube from the side of his chest, so I glimpsed the area of the incision—a huge, blue-purple swale of bruises up and down his swollen left side. No wonder his face contorts with every movement. He hugs a pillow in front of him as a brace to splint himself when he coughs. The doctor pulled out what looked like yards of tape— packing from the tracheostomy at the base of his neck— exposing that open mouth of a wound to the air so it can heal.

Harold can't speak at all. When he mouths words that I can't understand, I put my ear down near his lips. But it's no good; no sound comes out. I guess only one silent question: "The future?" I stall, giving him non-answers like, "My darling, we're in God's hands." And I wonder to myself what that means.

The tension lies in working to bolster Harold's faith and hope, and dealing honestly with my own lack. His belief in God's will and ways have always been rock-like; but I am a natural skeptic. A Scripture reading yesterday mentioned "filling up any little cracks there may yet be in your faith." Cracks? They're yawning crevasses.

✱ Next morning I could only stay with Harold in ICU for a few minutes. In the afternoon, though, I was allowed to stay in his room for several hours, holding his hand with my left hand, editing with my right when not helping him clear his trach. tube (pronounced *trāke*) or giving him rubs. I'm realizing what a huge dimension of being together is lost when you can't talk.

✱ Thursday I got the final report from pathology; the tumor is "papillary mucinous-secreting adenocarcinoma," exactly what the surgeon had predicted. In plain language, lung cancer of an aggressive type. The doctors will tell Harold. But then, together, we must look this damnable fact squarely in the face. The weather has turned cold.

✱ Jeff slept about two hours at home before meeting me at the hospital, his little Rabbit packed full for his trip east. He'll drive all night. H. and I both feel he should go. He must not put his life on hold. It's a great opportunity to work in New York as a trader on the Stock Exchange. He told his father good-bye in ICU. So downcast, all of us. Jeff, tender and distraught at leaving. He comforted me all the way down to the parking lot, where we said our good-byes. His presence, his arm around me, his shoulder next to mine felt so close and loving, and now one more strut in our human support system is gone, though John, Robin, and Marian Kussro (our second daughter, who lives with her family in Indianapolis) call almost every night.

✱ Kris and I were eating French toast this morning when the phone rang. What new crisis was upon us? Then I heard a nurse's dulcet voice: "Mrs. Shaw, would you pick up some grape popsicles on your way over this morning? Harold doesn't like our lemon or banana pops!"

Would I? Within ten minutes I was at the local grocery where I found lemon-grape striped popsicles. Harold sucked on one with difficulty but also with something approaching enthusiasm.

The nurses are annoyed about all the flowers which have been arriving in groves but are not allowed in ICU and have been collecting at the nurses' station. Most of the plants are large and growing.

Their weight and size meant several trips as I moved them home in the car. Our house is beginning to look like a rain forest.

✱ My mind often sees golden words that seem to hang in the air to color and describe our lives. The word written over today: "Wait."

Though H. is out of ICU and in an Intermediate Care room, he is weak, tired, in great pain, and today he was unable to meet my eye or squeeze my hand. Why? Are the questions in his mind too great to bear? Cut off from him by his pain, I dissolved in tears.

Kathy and Tom Burrows came to visit, and talking to them in the waiting room steadied my emotions so that I was able to go back in with them, more in control. Kathy told Harold he looked so manly, her complimentary way of describing his unshampooed hair and unshaven chin. The atmospheric tension eased.

After they left, H. and I "talked" for a while via mouthed words, and pen and clipboard. This new room has a sunny, pleasant outlook and less hardware. In ICU Harold had seemed like a mere appendage to all the mechanical support systems and monitors.

✱ This morning I found Harold sitting up! He was alert and strong enough to look through the month's bills and help me understand them. I shaved him, and supported him as he walked, shakily, to the bathroom. He wrote "I feel ancient." Yet later I called his room from the office and he answered it himself. His trach. tube had been taken out and he sounded almost normal!

Later I wrote some thank-you notes amid constant phone calls, then took off again for the hospital. Harold, feeling much stronger, said, "You're so beautiful." His eyes filled with tears as he looked up at me. I threw down my coat and we hugged. It's hard to hug fiercely and gently at the same time. I have rarely felt so vulnerable, so bittersweetly close.

✱ Dr. Parker tells us that radiation is ineffective for Harold's kind of cancer. It feels as though the deck is stacked against us. Why? *God, there must be something we can do beyond just waiting.*

But *wait* is the command we must obey whether we want to or not. Perhaps, if we're stripped of human resources, God will intervene, and do what doctors can't. We are praying along those lines. "Wait on the Lord, be of good courage." It's the same message that comes to me in slow surges in my dark search for heart-level faith. This is a long, underground passage. Struggle forward, wait as help comes, and the light will begin to glimmer. Won't it?

Three

As I parked in front of the dry cleaner's yesterday a man in a pick-up truck said, "You'd better watch that front tire, lady, it's getting low." "But it's a radial," I protested. "Yeah, but it's running on the sides." I pulled out the Peugeot Owners Manual, found the optimum tire pressure, and pumped it up at Auto-Ade. I can't help making a connection between this slow leakage, this gasping out of air, and Harold's lung and the leak through his trach. incision. Air, life, spirit, breath. Am I being shown something? Will the slow leak persist, flatten the tire, deflate the lung? How long can we keep pumping it up?

* When I read Scripture passages aloud to Harold each day, I find I tend to skip the parts that refer to entering heaven or being prepared for eternity. I guess I don't want us to see such verses as omens of coming death, even though they're meant to be promises of life. But death has to be died first, before the life in heaven can be lived. Maybe those verses are there as a real preparation—to run our thinking into a new channel.

Now I feel calmer. But is this serenity a shield against something that lies ahead? I keep trying to arm myself against future assault. Marian and the babies are coming from Indianapolis tonight. I look forward urgently to having them, to feeling their arms around my neck.

✱ While Marian cleaned up my sewing room chaos this morning, I went to the hospital, shampooed Harold's hair and washed his back, noticing with relief that the swelling of his incision is reduced and the bruise along his left side is almost unnoticeable. Kerrie, his "best nurse," gave me a crash course in changing his tracheostomy dressing, which I'll be doing at home until it is healed.

The plan now is for him to come home Saturday, so I'm cleaning our bedroom, washing all our bed linens and towels, and removing the inevitable piles of books, magazines, and manuscripts which have grown up like skyscrapers from all our tables and chairs during the month H. has been in hospital.

How full can one day be filled? The house is disorderly with the sticky, spreading disorder that characterizes the presence of small children. Planted one of Harold's hospital mum plants in the garden, then picked a bowl of tomatoes and green peppers for Megs, my assistant editor. Started a load of laundry. Went through several large cartons and bags of clothes destined for the thrift shop. Then off to the office.

Harold phones—a little desperate at the thought of another day and night in the hospital. The doctor has approved his discharge. He wants me to come and get him—*now,* this morning!

"Of course," I tell him, "Sure, we can do it. Great! Get them to go ahead with all your discharge paperwork; set the wheels in motion."

What a party we make as we leave the hospital! Six pillows,

cartons of medications, dressings, flowers, cards, books, tapes. H. is moved, even weepy, to be actually coming home. I simply feel an overwhelming contentment to have him sitting beside me in the car.

Marian has soup ready, and he eats lunch, sitting on the couch while opening the mail, including the fourth letter from Madeleine L'Engle since his illness. Her letters are forthright, cheerful, compassionate.

Getting Harold upstairs is tough, slow, with several pauses for breath. Now he's in bed, arranged amid a bevy of pillows.

His tracheostomy is still leaking. It sounds like the air whooshing out of a squashed balloon and makes the effort of speaking or coughing twice as hard for him because half of the air is lost through the gap in his throat rather than channeling past vocal chords, tongue, and lips. The wound will heal from the edges in, and eventually seal itself off.

✱ Getting ready for bed and climbing in with Harold and his five pillows is marvelous. To be close again, able to talk and touch and feel together is like a banquet after an enforced fast. Lauren comes in to say "Good night, Grampa" in her pajamas and kisses us each. Arms folded on the edge of the bed, dark eyes serious, she says gravely, "I'm praying for you."

✱ As it turned out, it was a difficult night, literally full of ups and downs. Harold couldn't get comfortable, accustomed as he was to the flexibility of a hospital bed. He panicked several times at the sensation of breathlessness and felt either too hot or too cold. Several times, just after getting to sleep, I had to wake, turn on the light, and try a new pillow arrangement. H. is worried about the pain in his chest, worried about everything. I guess he thought coming home would solve all his problems, be pure heaven, and lo and behold, he's still beset with pain and weakness and a tired wife who struggles with being on call twenty-four hours a day!

✳ Friday night's restlessness has become Saturday's chaos. I am feeling frustration at the mess at home. Everything seems out of control. I realize how much I like order. Our house is not designed for a sick person, nor is it baby-proof any longer. There's so much washing and food preparation and running up and down stairs, filling little requests from H. *I want* to write thank-you notes for all the flowers and visits, *want* to get the pile of editing done, *want* to write in this journal. I especially want to help Marian sew the bathrobe for Harold, which I had cut out for him two Christmases ago but have never finished— until I realize how much it means to her to have something tangible to do for her dad.

Mark, my son-in-law, and his brother Kurt, arrive from Batavia at 9:30 ready for work—replacing the garage windows, fixing the sagging porch, cleaning gutters and putting in storm windows. It's worth a lot to me to have the physical repairs completed. But there's much inner, emotional damage that needs mending, and that's not so easily fixed.

✳ Harold started the day by waking at 4 A.M., feeling bogged down under all the real and potential problems we face. I had decided last night to take the day off and stay home, catching up with myself, my thoughts, my feelings, and allowing the aching fatigue a chance to flow away. We lay in bed together after breakfast, and cried.

Outside was dense fog. Inside my mind I felt fogged in,

realities invisible. Caught in my own melancholy, I called David Mains, and within half an hour he was at our house. How good to have a friend to cry with freely, without embarrassment. He read the whole letter of *Philippians* aloud and prayed with us and we discussed the weight of family and business decisions in the light of an unknown future. David suggested that we need an advisory board for our business.

Later, Eric came and read Psalm 4, commenting with his usual cogent wisdom. We prayed together at length. Harold thinks that Psalm 118:17 was meant for him: "You shall live and not die."

✳ The Wheaton Writers Conference is on. I heard Frederick Buechner say in Chapel something I needed to hear: "If you beat a path to God long enough, he will come to you on the path you have beaten, bringing you the gift of himself." It reminded me of Psalm 50:23: "To him who uses praise over and over again—enough to make a trodden path—to him [her] will I show my deliverance."

✳ Harold no longer has to hold a gauze pad over his throat in order to speak. His wound is healed, all but a little whistlehole of a vent. I took him for a drive through Wayne, his first outing since leaving the hospital.

As he sat in the car I photographed the damp, mild colors of Illinois in Fall—golds, mostly, with some scarlet firebush and sumac. In spite of (or because of) the transient loveliness of the country, Harold came in from the car despondent. "My life is so *jolted*," he said slowly. "Why lung cancer?" And it seems just as unreal to me—purely irrational. Harold has never smoked; his health has always been sturdy. In the face of his

33

chronic well-being and clean living, this malignant disease is outrageous. I can't help thinking of all the people who smoke all their lives and seem to escape the consequences.

✱ I see Harold's strength inching back. The trach. wound is stitching itself up cell by cell without needle or thread as I clean and dress it twice a day. Today he went up and downstairs about four times, showing John Deck, my visiting brother, which storm windows need repairing and fitting in place. It's amazing how much contentment and security it gives H. to know that the house is tight against winter—gutters mended, furnace checked—yet what a frail protection a house is when the enemy may be eating away inside the walls, destroying us from within.

Some lines from Eve Perrera's poem, "Farm Animals in Winter," tell of other creatures—cows and horses—that must endure the immobility and cold of winter. She asks:

> Could I do it if I had to,
> Face some grim existence, stolid,
> nostrils to the wind?
>
> We'll only know when we get there,
> when we face the wintry places,
> what's the center we are made of,
> and the wintry places look
> much closer now.
>
> Beyond them lies the only valid barn.

The words frame the challenge Harold and I must face in the months to come. As Paul Parker has said to us twice: "We are all terminal."

Four

In a sense sickness is a place," writes Flannery O'Connor, "more instructive than a trip to Europe." It's true. There's an emotional landscape that changes within the days, much as one range of hills disappears when the next is approached. And it is a fascinating landscape, for all of its rocky wildness. This week's bleak outlook is like a winter climate which teaches mind and spirit and body new truths. I feel sad because hope has been diminished. At the same time I feel detached and isolated. It has been hard to talk intimately with Harold about his cancer and his future. I don't want my disillusion to color his view of this new country we are entering. I want to comfort and warm him. But I need comfort and warmth myself.

My recourse is poetry. This is what I wrote during the night:

Questions:

Beside me, under the sheet, his shape
is blurred, his breath irregular, racing
or slowing to the stress/release
of dreams. One lung—a wing of air—

has been already clipped. The scans
show the dark shadows on his bones.

His house of cells—blue-printed
by heredity, assembled season
by season (the greyed wood
shrinking a little at the joints
under the wash of time and storm)
—will it collapse like a barn
settling into its field? His spirit—
iridescent as a pigeon feather—
will it escape before mine
through a break in the roof,
homing, homing through the sky?

("*Our days . . . quickly pass,
and we fly away*" Ps. 90:10.)

✻ Harold's prayer before a meal, square head bowed, strong
hand holding mine, "Lord, we thank you for this day," has new
meaning. Every day has uniqueness when the sum of them is
finite.

Last night we walked the half-mile circuit down St. Charles,
to Morningside, to Wynn, to Fair Oaks and back home in the
crystal brilliance of the perfectly still Fall evening—every leaf
and barn and fence post cleanly outlined and real in itself.

✻ A return to normalcy. Only one Tylenol tablet and one
pillow at night, and Harold seems well enough for me to be
gone twenty-four hours.

I rose at 4:45 A.M. and headed east for Bowling Green
University in Ohio for the Conference on Christianity and

Literature where I had a paper to give on the poetry of C. S. Lewis. Harold has been worried about the Peugeot, and I called him as soon as I reached the motel.

I felt rather nervous about my paper, "Looking Back to Eden," and was last to read, but got a warm response from Tom Howard. In his own paper Tom asked: "Is autobiography a form of hubris? How can we really know and tell the truth about ourselves?" Such questions move from the rhetorical to the real as I write this journal. *God, I need to know from you whether or not I am telling the truth about myself.*

✱ A week's worth of recollection: I left Harold for a day and a half, and returned exhilarated.

By some trick of light or atmosphere all the foliage along the highway, which seemed dull on the drive east, is now ardent with color. I especially love the glimpses of small maple saplings growing between much larger trees in the stands of heavy forest. You see them for one moment only at 65 miles per hour—flaming with pink-red-scarlet—and then they're gone, but today they're still burning in my mind.

I am so shaken by the beauty of shapes and colors. The contours of a half-harvested cornfield, poplars with leaves left only at their tips, the gleam of light on water, ducks and geese. As I turn into our driveway, our little maple tree shows golden, more so than I have ever seen it, with an inner glow, even though the sky is overcast. It's a tree that has always seemed to try to be bright but has always failed. Maybe it is finding itself at last.

✱ The mail keeps piling in. A letter from Paula D'Arcy moved me to tears. She had spent a whole day at her beach cottage on Long Island Sound, praying for Harold and reading my poetry aloud. She said she felt close to us there. We spent four golden days with her just this time last year.

✱ With John and Joan McDermott, Joan fully recovered for years from her cancer, we have an hour and a half of conversation and prayer. It is reinforcing. Dinner becomes unimportant. In the flow of words with reality behind them (they have both known major surgery, both have faced death), we feel a vital union with them. My question: Should we take the initiative and ask believing friends like these to come regularly and pray, or should we wait for them to suggest it? It seems presumptuous for us to interrupt their lives with our demands. But for us it is literally a matter of life and death.

After supper Kris reads aloud to us from a book of Scripture readings. The theme for the evening reading centers on the degree to which Christ enters into our human experience. We discuss how the Shekinah glory penetrated the tabernacle and temple (though none of us can recall when the glory *left*— maybe in Ezekiel?). It strikes me that the New Testament counterpart of the Shekinah glory was the tongues of fire resting on the heads of the disciples—the Holy Spirit coming to inhabit humans rather than a building. David cried out in anguish in Psalm 51, "Take not your Holy Spirit from me." Even if the flame of the Spirit doesn't desert us, if we damp him down, snuff him with our bushel basket of doubt, may we render God invisible in us?

George MacDonald, in spite of extraordinary privation— death, disease, poverty, rejection—shone with the life of Christ. Perhaps that's what stress and pain are meant to do— trim the wick, sharpen the light.

✳ A packet of vine bark has arrived by air mail from a missionary friend in Peru. He claims its efficacy as a cancer cure. Each strip of bark is to be shredded, then boiled and steeped to produce a brew to be drunk four times a day. We don't know what to do about it. Should we get going with it right away, or wait to talk to the oncologist?

Perhaps we'll ask her tomorrow, when we see her for the first time—Dr. Liz Hillman. We are hoping for answers—some definitive plan, specific steps to take, an overview of future possibilities and probabilities. That may be too much to ask of one human, however expert.

✳ At the clinic today the thoracic surgeon who operated on Harold orders two post-op x-rays of H.'s chest, and after examining him, is obviously pleased with his own artwork. The right lung is clear, the healing of the incision complete. Harold still has scatters of staples in him where blood vessels were clamped off after his left lung was removed. It's funny to see these on the x-rays, like a stapled pile of correspondence.

We feel encouraged. Harold lost eleven pounds in the hospital, but since then has gained one back. To me he looks attractively slim, though still a little droopy from the residual weakness.

After a quick lunch at home we set off for the university hospital where Liz Hillman has her office. It's a huge medical complex—so many buildings, so many staff, so many patients—but somehow it feels a bit more comfortable because our son John was a medical student here for three years.

After giving H. a thorough going-over, Liz announces that she has some concerns about the bone scans on which the various "hot spots," like the ribs, show plainly. She orders another scan (next Tuesday), plus a CT (Computerized

Tomography) scan of liver, lungs, and mediastinum, also another CEA blood test, which is done before we leave.

✳ At the Wade Lecture tonight I introduced Rolland Hein who read a letter written by George MacDonald to his daughter Mary. She had expressed concern that she didn't *feel* enough love for God (which so often is exactly my problem). Her father said that there are three requisites for a loving relationship: That the persons involved be capable of loving, that they be themselves lovable, and that they know each other.

For me, it's the last item that is shadowed. How can I know an invisible, inaudible, intangible presence? Through the Word and the Spirit, of course. To my mind steeped in evangelicalism, the orthodox theology springs into place almost automatically. But time is needed, quiet, for the voice of God to be heard, the relationship to be cultivated. And I have none, unless I short-change the people in my life. I think I hear God saying to me, "*I'm* being short-changed. Don't you care?"

✳ Breakfast at the Mains with the Group. We feel warmed by the love of these friends, who pray for H. before we eat. I find myself saying to them, "In spite of the pain and crisis, we've had a wonderful two months together."

I'm amazed by the equanimity with which I can sometimes view life. I can laugh and kid around and it's not a front. I feel tired often, but somehow excited today to be living through this uncertainty with Harold and even anticipating more of the same. It's like a cosmic adventure.

✻ Sunday I saw a lovely growth of Virginia creeper on the stone church wall by the back entrance, a pinky, opaque peach color almost the shade of the stone itself. Longed for my camera.

For the second time in a row, Rick omitted a part of the liturgy which has great meaning for me, the words just before Communion, when he presents the bread and wine, saying, "The gifts of God for the people of God. Take them in remembrance that Christ died for you, and feed on him in your hearts by faith, with thanksgiving." I let him know that those words are important to me, and that I would say them in my heart even if he doesn't use them!

In the evening we attended the St. Mark's Inquirer's class, an informal group of about twenty who meet to discuss the basics of the Christian's life and belief. It's funny to be an inquirer into things you have known all your life—funny, but salutary. Both Harold and I, with our Plymouth Brethren background, are ingrained with biblical truths from long exposure. But for me it was too often truth dried out into a kind of flat legalism which has dropped away behind us since we started coming to St. Mark's last year.

Karen and David are also in the class. Afterwards, I ask them to pray for Harold. Karen puts her whole self into this kind of prayer, hands pressed over Harold's back and chest.

It is wonderful how so many of our friends have begun to pray with us regularly. The McDermotts, the Bosches, Eric, Karen and David—all have plunged into prayer with us as if our lives depended on it! They do.

✻ Today a bone scan is scheduled for H. at the university hospital complex, which means an early start, difficult for him.

After we enter the bowels of the huge edifice where John did so much of his training, we have to wait in the crowded, smoky waiting room while a new batch of radio-active material is mixed for Harold's injection. Then a three-hour hiatus while the stuff circulates in his system and is taken up by his bones. During the scan he must lie flat on a hard table, motionless, for nearly an hour. By the time it is over he is stiff and shaking with fatigue. He feels no pain, only claustrophobia.

Driving home, I am suddenly struck with the huge and unanswerable question, "Why does my husband have lung cancer?" We seem to be handling it well and then some random thought, like a pipe sunk to an aquifer, brings to the surface the imponderable and all its implications.

✳ Thursday we return to the hospital for the CT scan and x-rays. The hospital's lower level is a rabbit warren, and navigating it is complicated by the fact that all the offices have just been shifted around and now no one knows where anyone else is. You get instructions like: "Uh, take the stairs to the lower level, then turn left and follow the red line to the end, then left again and right at the elevators. I think that's where Radiology is now."

The scan itself takes over an hour. I watch most of it on the screen as the great white doughnut of a machine does its computer-assisted tomography of Harold's torso, slice by eighth-inch slice. It is fascinating to watch one image of his secret interior slide off the screen to be replaced by the next.

The soft tissues seem to be clear of cancer, though the skeletal "hot spots" have yet to be evaluated. From both Dr. Hillman and Dr. Parker we learn that the CEA blood test shows the tumor factor down from 16 to 6.2. Still no result on the most recent CEA test done last Friday.

✱ Gave Saturday morning breakfast to three friends of John McDermott, Jr. who drove out from Chicago to pray for Harold. Later on they started to pray for me, for the tension in my neck, for my doubts. Since I felt no change and saw nothing happening in my thinking they left, discouraged. For my part, I felt like a failure, as if surely with enough faith I could have worked up something better for them.

This afternoon I was down—one of my periodic attacks of agnosticism. I shared my depression with Harold, feeling guilty because I should be encouraging him, not loading him with more problems. He tried to comfort me though, as he always does. I cried desperately up in our bedroom.

Why can't I feel or see God, or sense his reality? Why is my imagination paralyzed in this area, where I need to be freest? Finally, I called John in Pensacola and spilled it all out to my emphathetic son who is so like me. He had no definitive answers, but relief came in expressing what I felt, and in being understood.

✱ Another wintry day, freezing, with a biting wind. Took my camera to church this morning to photograph the vine on the wall, but the leaves had all fallen. Only the woody stalk was left, clinging to the stone.

This morning Rick included in the liturgy the words I had talked to him about: "The gifts of God for the people of God . . . feed on him in your hearts by faith, with thanksgiving." His inclusion of them today was like a special gift to me.

✱ Our Peugeot—that silver-blue French beauty Harold just couldn't resist—needs servicing (she always needs something), so we get up early, drive both cars to LaGrange, and leave her there. The blueness and stillness of the day are so intense that we cannot just rush back to the office, but meander into Hinsdale, past Graue Mill and the "scary place," where the road seems to run almost into Salt Creek.

On impulse, we turn into the little Bronswood Cemetery, full of old trees and old gravestones. We asked ourselves a couple of days ago about buying cemetery lots, and decided Yes. Now here we are, in our "favorite" cemetery, surrounded by firs and russet oaks. We sit on the grass, warm, feeling the rightness of making this choice together, planning it in a moment of peace and calm, not waiting to be overcome by all the stark possibilities that lie ahead. We have never felt closer.

✱ Some new poems are coming fast. It is hard to interrupt their birth with the banalities of editing, but life is always a mix of sapphires and garlic. I sent off one new poem to Maxine Hancock, whose letter inspired it:

The comforting

She said she heard the sound
for the first time
that evening

They were walking the back pasture
to river-edge
not talking, taking in
the half-moon, breathing the
lucid silence, when at their left
a wind seemed to lift and he said
"listen" and "there they are"

And she saw that the wind-sound
was wing-sound, that a cloud of ducks

was moving the sky. Without
a cry the pulse of two hundred
feathered wings
shook the whole night

She knew then
how the Comforter had sounded—
the strong breath of his arrival,
the Spirit wing-beat
filling their ears

And knowing our need of comfort
in a dark, chill night
she folded the sound into words
in a little card
and sent it to us with her love

Five

I am pressured by impulses I can't fulfill, books I have no time to read, the urgencies of meals and manuscripts and gas pumps and high school carpools. Sometimes I can't think a thought through to its conclusion. The phone is shrill, impossible to ignore. And I depend on it; the need to talk is addictive; I am compelled to stay close to family and friends in these days and letters take too long to write, or send. I am surrounded by people and stimuli and work, but my soul is so lonely. I cry and cry to God to come by me and I suppose, in some unseen, unprovable way he does, but the Presence is not immediate enough to bring comfort—it's like taking half an aspirin for a migraine. Other people seem to feel his warmth and reality, and are not filled with sharp questioning.

"You speak in my heart and say, 'Seek my face.' Your face, Lord, will I seek" (Ps. 27:8). A face is a person's most identifiable personal feature. When two are face to face, the eyes spark, the lips move, the tongue articulates, the ears listen. There is a frontal intimacy. I seek that face that will look into mine and say, "You are real. I acknowledge you."

But "O, tarry and wait for the Lord's pleasure" (v. 14). That word *wait* again.

✻ I was not prepared for Liz Hillman's evening call, telling us that H.'s CEA test now shows a factor of 27 instead of dropping as we had hoped. It shook us both. We tried to talk on the phone with her about the implications, but she insisted that we must discuss the options in person. We have an appointment Monday. "It's funny," Harold remarked later, "but I feel as well now as at any time since surgery."

Then John and Joan came to pray. The prophetic word for H. tonight was that he has a deep valley to go through but will climb out the other side. Unvoiced, the questions burn in me: Is it the valley of struggle, or the valley of death's shadow? Is the "other side" earth or heaven?

✻ What a comfort! Jeff drove in at 3:00 A.M. from New York! I asked him if he is happy. He said he feels contented with his job, grateful for the friends he's connected with in the area, and exhilarated by the adventure of living away from home and surviving. "Happy" is not the applicable word. His affection and tenderness are like a warm sweater on a chilly day.

✻ Today has been labeled "Very Important" in my mind for the last ten days. At eight o'clock we drive down in brilliant sunlight for our consult with Dr. Hillman. Promptly at 9 we knock on a series of locked doors in the special hematology section of the lower level, when out pops Liz's head and we are drawn into the cluttered, overflowing office she shares with another doctor.

She reviews all the data gathered and while she cannot categorically claim that the bone shadows and the small spots on the right lung are cancer, she suspects active tumor growth somewhere in Harold's body, because of the rising figures of the CEA blood test. She outlines three chemotherapy regimens, and although none seems to give more than a twenty-five percent chance of therapeutic benefit, she recommends that he get started on one of them.

I tell her about all our praying friends, and the couples—the Bosches, the Thurmans, the McDermotts, Karen and David— committed to praying with us for healing regularly, on different nights of the week. "How do you feel about prayer for healing?" I ask. "I think it's great," she says, but mentions someone whose faith was destroyed when such prayer was not rewarded by healing. She even goes so far as to admit that maybe the Lord is already intervening—that Harold is an atypical lung cancer patient. He has good color, is gaining weight and energy, is feeling good, has no cancer pain. In fact, his adenocarcinoma seems to be "indolent," a word I find charming. She means by that that the cancer doesn't seem to be wildly aggressive, as demonstrated by the very slow changes, or lack of changes, on the scans of the last two and a half months.

It seems a shame to interrupt this felicitous state, so she agrees to wait, to check Harold again December 15, and to postpone a decision about chemotherapy until then. The consultation ends with a warm hug for us both. More x-rays and blood tests are scheduled for December.

✱ Driving home from the office these days, on crystal clear evenings, I've noticed that after the sun has set, for a while the light and color seem to intensify. Tonight an extraordinarily vivid rose-gold, like the red wedding-ring gold from Wales, flushes the Western sky. The spiky or feathery black silhouettes of trees and bushes and fields against this backdrop, along North Avenue or St. Charles Road, are so striking. There is film in the car, but by the time I get home and load the camera, it is too dark.

✱ Thanksgiving Day. A quiet day, turkey dinner at home preceded by a good walk with Harold and long-distance calls from all our kids.

I find it strange how sometimes the reality of cancer recedes, turns shadowy and distant. In the company of friends, we laugh and talk as if all were well, as if our lives were under control. At other times, the horror comes so close it bruises your chin and squeezes the breath out of you.

I want to believe that things will move along evenly and predictably. Kris must be feeling this too—the need for a safe sameness. But she can't talk about it.

✱ Kris and I saw *Amadeus* Friday afternoon—a movie full of beauty, horror, and death. Kris was quiet all the way home. I asked her what she'd thought of it and she said merely, "It was good." Later, I was irritated by her lack of helpfulness, her mute obstructiveness, and asked what was bothering her. "Nothing!"

Then we talk about a party we've been invited to the weekend before Christmas Day. I tell her we can't go, we'll probably be celebrating Christmas that weekend, not on Christmas Day itself because Jeff can be here only for the weekend. "Well, I'm going to wait till Christmas to open *my* presents," she insists. I tell her, in my best motherly accents, that we need to consider what is best for everyone and not be selfish. "Why are you so crabby?" I ask her mutinous face. She leaves the kitchen in a storm of tears. I follow her, hold her, hug her, imploring her to tell me what is wrong. "No one's acting the way they always have." I can see why any shift in pattern or routine is threatening to her—the tip of a shadow that is beginning to engulf her life—change too big to be believed, uncertainty impossible to acknowledge by talking about it.

Harold and I sit on each side of her on the couch while she sobs and sobs. He asks her, "Can you ask the Lord to help you accept changes, help you understand that life is always moving, but he moves with it?" She nods. We both pray for her, and I think she feels some relief. Her cheerfulness and helpfulness lighten the rest of the evening. And helping Kris to pray helps me.

✱ A notable event—attending the final Inquirer's class Sunday afternoon. Rick gives us a short introduction to liturgy and the use of the Book of Common Prayer. Then he passes around a sign-up list for those desiring to be confirmed December 9. Harold and I are sitting across the room from each other, having arrived too late to get seats together. We have no chance to confer on this, nor have we really discussed why we've been coming to the class, beyond a certain curiosity, and wanting to respond to Rick's invitation. The list comes to me first. After some hesitation I check the "Yes" column and pass it on. Later, driving to the Bosches for prayer, we look at each other, with an unspoken question. "'Yes,' was my answer," says Harold. "And mine." This brings us both relief, and gladness. Though I want very much to join this body of Christ, I don't want to move ahead of Harold. To discover that his desire coincides with mine, and mine with his, is an evidence of grace and miracle to us both.

✱ Yet Monday has been a dark day of depression—a thundercloud heavy with rain, boiling up from my horizon. I feel exhausted, weak, and overpowered. The approach of Christmas with all the planning for our family gathering, the social activities, plus the medical picture—I can hardly face it.

I give way to a flood of tears in bed. Harold is strong—praying with me and encouraging me with his own special brand of comfort. In our marriage this antiphonal balance almost always works; when one is down, the other is up.

I suppose I must be feeling *anomie*—the angst that has no name. Walker Percy talks about "the terrors of the night," those formless fears which are all the more devastating because we cannot pin them down. Perhaps the only solution to such darkness is similarly non-rational, or supra-rational—the prayer in tongues. At such times it seems my only release, that and clinging to Scriptures like planks in a rough sea. Like Philippians 4:6–7: "Have no anxiety, but in everything by prayer and humble entreaty express your needs to God, and his peace that passes understanding [is supra-rational] will suffuse *heart* and *mind*." I know I need solitude, quiet time alone—the meditation and contemplation that produce physical results as well as spiritual advances.

Even as I write this at 4:30 A.M., being unable to sleep, warmed by the kerosene heater in the family room, I recognize the gift of the uninterrupted, darkened hours. Mind is creating—darting off in several directions, planning, connecting, seeing through problems with a sense of anticipation that cancels out the early dull fatigue and numbness.

* Robin calls Tuesday afternoon, feeling lonely, needing a friend, needing the presence of God. She has been wanting to call me for three days; my burden has been increasing for the same three days. Has it been a kind of burden-bearing, or sharing between us, without our even knowing it? I don't know, but at the end of our conversation I pray with her and suddenly the pressure is lifted from both of us. Thousands of miles apart, we have the intimacy of prayer together.

It reminds me of our conversation with John last weekend.

From his Florida end of the phone, he said, "I'm looking at the new moon. She's so beautiful. Is the sky clear there? Go to the window and look." And we looked, and found comfort, a thousand miles away from each other, in seeing the fingernail of light together.

✸ Tuesday was significant for H. and me. Eric came for supper and prayed with his usual fervor and insight. Then we were joined by Mark Taylor and Lars Dunberg for two and a half hours of discussion about the future direction, and the options, for our publishing company. They have agreed to meet with us regularly as an advisory board. What a gift to have these friends—publishers, astute businessmen as well as visionaries—to bear our burden with us. They warned us that I may have to make future decisions about the company without Harold.

Lars suggested that we need to do some estate planning, and yesterday we consulted with two lawyers who are expert in that kind of thing.

A letter came from John McDermott, Jr. yesterday, telling us that if we need him he will fly from Cairo any time, and giving us his phone number. (He and Betsy are there, employed by Eastman Kodak.) H. and I sat at the lunch table, and tears ran down our faces as we read this. Yesterday John's father came to the office to pray with us. He gave us 2 Chronicles 15:7: "But you, take courage! Don't let your hands be weak, for your work shall be rewarded."

✸ One reason for my difficulty sleeping early this morning was the compulsion, like a command from the Lord, to get up and prepare the medicinal drink from the bark sent us from

Peru. I followed directions: shredded two foot-long strips of bark, brown as cinnamon sticks, and tough. I boiled the fibers in water for twenty minutes. The result was an acrid, dark-red concoction which I have sweetened with honey and flavored with lemon for greater palatability. Now Harold will have to decide if he wants to drink it.

Then it was sunrise—the cloud feathers brighter than a flamingo's. I photographed it just as the pink faded and gold flooded trees and grass against the contrast of leaden clouds in the west. This scene was perfectly echoed on FM radio with the playing of Brahms' Trio No. 3 with its intensity, agitation, fervor, awakening.

* We are now in Advent. The readings in the Lectionary start back at the beginning again. The Christmas tree has been bought. From where I write I can see it through the sliding door of the family room, sitting on the porch with the first snow sifting through it. The house, which is being transformed with Christmas decorations, is in chaos, like a woman caught in the middle of doing her hair.

Harold has been drinking his bark tea, though rather irregularly. It is bitter and makes him belch. I sent Dr. Hillman a brochure about another cancer treatment popular in the Bahamas. Over the phone she responded predictably, "Garbage!"

* I woke at 2:30 A.M. to the thought of the church as a ship, triggered by my new understanding of the word *nave,* from the latin *navis* (a ship). Wrote this:

GOD IN THE DARK

Hymn for St. Mark's Episcopal Church

Lord of all sailors, ships and sea,
Go with us over Galilee.

We leave behind our shelter'd cove
And venture forth Thy power to prove.

Our valiant voyagers, row on row,
Have filled this nave from stern to prow.

Through starless night and fearful gale,
Lord, with Thy help we will prevail,

Or if in breathless calm we fail,
Wind of the Spirit, fill our sail!

Our Pioneer and Pilot Thou,
Thy care has kept us safely. Now,

May our small ship so steady move
Across the surface of Thy love

That in the end safe harbor we
May reach in Thine eternity.

The moon was riding high and silver in the western sky. One hour and a rough hymn later, she had sunk to the horizon, sagging and yellow as a tired balloon. Back to bed, then up again to drive the carpool.

✱ Turning into Van Kampen's drive to pick up Karla for school, I saw the sun coming up behind a tangle of trees. Most of the landscape was still in shadow, but where St. Charles

54

Road merges with North Avenue, a round mouth of light opened—the sun shining through the throat of the road there, then looping toward me down a single telephone line. It was an epiphany—the arrival of light—but so brief, so fleeting.

Six

The obstinate weather blob, which has been stuck like gum over the Midwest, has finally dissipated; the sun is out. Got up early and photographed our mantlepiece with the sunlight striking across brick and copper and pewter. Also tried an out-of-focus shot of my cut-glass bottle stoppers in the sun, trying to retain the brilliance of color in those lovely hexagonal refractions that a camera makes of light.

Taking photos of the morning sunlight gives my day a good start. Light is dependable, yet so infinitely varied—the same each day, yet every day different. Like God, maybe? Perhaps that's why he shows us himself in the metaphor of light.

✱ We missed our prayer time with the McDermotts last night. Harold attended Living Bibles International board meetings all day, and together we had dinner with the board members. Sat with John Bolten who extolled the holistic approach to cancer treatment. He recently met a German doctor who believes that "ninety percent of cancer is caused by infection in the teeth and jaw," which invades the immune system. I had also talked to a friend in the afternoon whose doctor was also German, and who, after several cancer-free years following surgery for colon cancer, is an ardent advocate of laetrile, "wohbenzymes," distilled water, vegetarian diet, and coffee enemas.

We find all this perplexing. Clearly there are people who seem to be rid of cancer after using these therapies, labeled quackery by traditional medicine. The choice seems to be between getting at the cancer cells and damaging the immune system with chemotherapy, or going out on a limb with a program which may leave the immune system intact, but which the medical community condemns, and which may be ineffective and waste precious time.

✳ Yesterday, Sunday, was our confirmation day at St. Mark's. Just before leaving for church, Harold had a sudden attack of agonizing pain that lasted about fifteen minutes. He went quite white and nearly passed out. I got two Tylenol and codeine tablets into him, à la Dr. Parker's earlier instructions, prayed over him, rubbed his back as he was sitting, leaning his head into me, and then the pain was suddenly over. We think it might have been his old kidney stone. My concern then was what the codeine might do to him. Might he doze off during the bishop's homily? Or keel over when he knelt down for the laying-on-of-hands? Neither of these dire possibilities happened.

At church there were thirty confirmands. During the service, each candidate knelt before the bishop in turn as he cupped our hands with his hands, looked into our eyes, and prayed, "Defend, O Lord, your servant [Luci] with your heavenly grace that she may continue yours forever, and daily increase in your Holy Spirit more and more, until she comes to your everlasting kingdom. Amen." Then he signed the cross on our foreheads with holy oil, gave us the buffet—a firm slap on the cheek, to remind us of the hardships of being Christ's disciples—and touched our lips with his closed fist. The words of the hymn which we sang afterwards reflected my exact feelings:

Redeemer, now I open wide
My heart to thee, here Lord abide.
Let me thy inner presence feel,
Thy grace and love to me reveal.

✱ Last night we were at the Bosches for dinner, Scripture songs, and prayer. I was amused by David Mains' forthright request: "Lord, please heal Harold completely so that we can use our energy in other directions for the kingdom." Karen prayed that God would "remove the shadows from Harold's bones."

I am learning the new textures and colors of love—from friends like the McDermotts who have their own anxieties and who joined us in prayer tonight. We four sat close, each feeling the others' pain and stress. And from Christ—while praying I had what might be called a vision—a clear, inward perception that I was standing at the foot of the cross, directly under Jesus' feet so that blood from his wounds was actually dripping onto me. I felt a burst of emotion, with tears, which is rare for me in prayer. The old Brethren hymn sang itself in my mind: "O Lamb of God, Thy bleeding wounds,/with cords of love divine/have drawn our wayward hearts to Thee/and linked our life with Thine."

Then Kris, coming to say good night, laid her head on Harold's shoulder, he sitting on the couch, she standing behind him, bending forward—a posture of love and longing which showed all she couldn't put into words.

Even our love-making has a new, tender quality.

* I'm writing now at the outpatient clinic waiting room.
Extraordinary news this morning. Harold called Dr. Parker
for the results of Tuesday's CEA blood test. Paul said, "It's very
puzzling. I called Liz Hillman as soon as I got the result and
it's most surprising." "Paul," Harold said with unusual
patience, "what *is* the result?" "The tumor factor is down to 1."
"What does that mean?" "Of course, we'll have to check it
again, but if it's a true reading, it's miraculous."
The Lectionary psalm for the day condenses all our hopes
into words:

> O Lord my God, I cried out to you,
> It is you who restore me to health.
> You brought me up, O Lord, from the dead;
> You restored my life as I was going down to
>   the grave.
> You have turned my wailing into dancing.
> You have put off my sackcloth and clothed me
>   with joy.
>
> Ps. 30:8–11

But Liz Hillman was disgusted with us when we admitted
the bark tea routine. "That really does muddy the waters," she
protested. "I thought this month was going to be a test of
prayer and that this would be the high point of my afternoon!"
I am beginning to see why she feels frustrated. *We* aren't likely
to be picky about how H. is cured—whether by prayer or
medicinal tea. But as a scientist Liz is not only interested in his
physical progress but in how it happens. In effect, what we did
was to reject her chemotherapy in favor of prayer and then, in
addition, adopt an unproven chemo regimen of our own.
H. asked her if it was unusual for a CEA reading to drop

without treatment. She rolled her eyes. "*Highly* unusual." She told us that if H. is in remission as a result of prayer, she wants it documented, which means more CT scans and bone scans. Though his chest x-rays show no changes, she now flatly describes his bones with their dark spots as "metastatic."

Even if Harold is healed, I don't want to (a) stop praying or (b) let up on good nutrition. The crisis seems to have eased, which could also ease our sense of dependence on God and his providence. We have been in the press of prayer and it's a good place to be. To return to the old easy acceptance of life, the taking for granted of health and wholeness, would be anticlimactic, a step backward.

✱ Yesterday we awoke to a light dusting of snow that covered the outside world. Last night a layer of frost was added. I drove the car pool to school and found the dazzle of sun on crystals irresistible. Shot some grasses arc-ing in the sun, sheathed in silver.

Robin, Mark, and Lindsay arrived later in the day from the West Coast for Christmas. Robin got to work immediately, cleaning the cabinets in my kitchen and organizing my neglected refrigerator. What a relief to have her, and her ready help!

About 8:30 P.M. Liz Hillman phoned. She said, "I'm sorry to call you so late." Me: "I'm sorry you have to work so late." Liz: "I'm sorry for another reason." My heart began to pound. "Is there a problem?" Liz: "Harold's CEA is up to 71." Silence. I called to H. to get on the other phone. Liz: "You're the last on my list. I didn't want to disturb you. I wanted to leave you feeling high for the holidays, but that wouldn't have been fair to you."

She thinks that somehow the lab mixed the labels on the earlier test, accounting for the false, low reading.

As we talked, Kris came and sat on the bed beside me and tucked her arm around me. I cocked the phone away from my ear so she could hear the conversation. We were both trembling. Liz suggested we get another CEA test from the clinic to see what results they find this time. And in January, another bone scan and CT scan. And chemotherapy? "I've said all along you should start it right away, while you're feeling good, before the disease has sapped your strength." "But it seems awful to interrupt that sense of well-being with chemo." "Yes. I understand how you feel. And I do think Harold's condition is remarkable. Adenocarcinoma often kills in eight months, and he must have had it at least that long—long before anyone guessed it was there. But we can't let it get away from us now."

After we hung up the phones, Harold came upstairs. Lying on our bed, we read again, aloud, the words of Psalms 103, 71, 91. We talked about the "pestilence that walks in darkness." We prayed, the three of us holding hands.

✱ Winter solstice, when the sun seems to stand still in heaven, watching for the Baby to be born.

John McDermott called early. Before hearing anything about yesterday's developments, he said, "I have a couple of verses for you. I feel so strongly they are for you, I had to call." The verses were from Hebrews 10:35–39: "Do not let your trust in the Lord die away, no matter what happens. . . . You need to patiently keep on doing God's will if you want him to do for you all that he has promised. . . . You must live by faith, trusting him in everything."

In spite of the return of the psychological pressure of knowing things are getting worse, we are both at peace this morning. H. is feeling well. We drove to work and he handed out the Christmas bonus checks to all our people, then went to the clinic for another test.

* Two moving letters today. One from Ruth El Saffar, a writer and professor at the University of Illinois, told what my poem "Judas, Peter" had meant to her when she was undergoing stress.

> because we are all
> betrayers, taking
> silver and eating
> body and blood and asking
> (guilty) is it I and hearing
> him say yes
> it would be simple for us all
> to rush out
> and hang ourselves
>
> but if we find grace
> to cry and wait
> after the voice of morning
> has crowed in our ears
> clearly enough
> to break our hearts
> he will be there
> to ask us each again
> do you love me

"Grace to cry and wait." Yes, that is what we all need. Another letter from Lois Lake Church, who found emotional healing following the death of her baby last April, and who has conceived again, told the part my poems had had in this process. That words written years ago seem to carry a power that has nothing to do with me, that my thought can jump to another's mind over a gap of years and miles with the printed page as a bridge, amazes me.

✳ Since Thursday H. has had pain in his right leg, jabs of it, with a steady ache in between. It's worrying. It could be a symptom from the metastatic spot on his pubic bone, sciatica, or just a pulled muscle.

✳ Christmas Eve started out with a silver snow that continued through the day. Harold's leg was painful, but Tylenol kept it under control. In the morning Dr. Parker called with the puzzling news that the last CEA reading, taken at the Glen Ellyn Clinic, was 29.2. So we have three readings in the past two weeks of 1, 71, and 29. It's like a lottery.

✳ Christmas Day. Bright, clear, minus three degrees. All the family are here but Jeff, who had to return to New York last night. We opened presents, and I took lots of photographs of the three little girls, our granddaughters who are finding out the fun of being cousins. They live too far apart to have that pleasure often.

After baked ham, we had cake in the family room. It seemed natural to suggest that we all pray for Harold. "But first," he said, "I want to read you some of the Bible passages that have come alive for me in the last few weeks." Harold is a good reader, but he struggled with the words and his emotions as he read. Then he prayed for each of us in the room, for the future mates of John, Jeff, and Kris, and for all our grandchildren, born and yet to be born, blessing us all in the name of Christ.

One by one, each of us was crying, out of our grief and incredulity, our sense of loss, pain, and fear. Kris lay sobbing on the couch, her feet in H.'s lap and her head in Marian's lap. It was a good, hard, precious, difficult, close, intense, unifying time. We all felt the pull between faith and reality—having faith for healing, yet not allowing ourselves to be devastated by *No* answers from God. Tentatively, someone suggested that perhaps healing would be in the ultimate sense—the return to wholeness in heaven.

A recent letter from David Alexander of Lion Publishing in England helped us: "In your situation, I hope I would be angry, not at God for allowing it and threatening your life together, but at the whole fallenness/frustration/evil of a world which has brought sickness and death upon itself. Jesus makes it clear that it is not our own personal sin which causes the tower to fall on us. But equally clearly it is the sin of the world, in which we are all bound up, which is the cause of sickness and death."

✱ December 29—my birthday. H. bought me a speaker-phone which allows everyone in the room to hear a conversation. Kris gave me a stainless steel saucepan. Earlier John had chosen and purchased some heathery yarn for me to knit into a sweater for myself.

This fifty-sixth year of mine has been full of change-points, unexpected spurts of growth, needle-eyes through which I have been pulled. The coming year is an unfilled blank. I have made few professional commitments; I can't risk them. All my energy is needed here. My centripetal pull is toward Harold, whose life is endangered and whose welfare is uncertain. Of one thing I feel certain—that 1985 will bring more dark uncertainty. All we can do is walk through it.

II

STRAINING TO SEE

January–April 1985

*No: a glimpse is not a vision. But to a
man on a mountain road by night, a
glimpse of the next three feet of road may
matter more than a vision of the horizon.*

—C. S. LEWIS, **letter to Sheldon Vanauken**

One

I stood at our window Saturday afternoon and looked west. The sun was low, shining along the surface of the deep snow. A strong wind flowed over the icy crust and carried snow particles along in its eddies. It made the wind visible in a curious and beautiful way, like a fast-moving river of light, the snow-dust catching and holding the glints from the sun. I think the Spirit (wind) of God is made visible in the individuals in our lifestream. God shines on them, and shows us in their lives the way the wind is moving.

* Sunday was clear, bright, and not too cold. We three went to church together for the first time in weeks. Afterwards everyone who saw Harold commented on how well he looks, how good his color. Are they just being kind, or do they really think he looks healthy? It's hard for me to tell anymore. He is thinner than before, walks more slowly, more deliberately and with caution, and often feels weak and breathless. It's strange that I need the eyes of friends to see my husband's condition.

The Bosches came to pray at four o'clock. Afterwards, Georgia's face was streaming with tears. She and Bernie really love us, and we them. It suddenly struck me what a commitment these and our other praying friends are making— not just to pray until healing is given, but to pray *even if healing isn't given*. It is working prayer; these friends give themselves in time, energy, emotional identification. They are part of us. It reminds me of the healing miracle in which virtue went out of Jesus. When he was touched by the woman with the issue of blood, some of his strength flowed into her. Our friends hurt because we hurt. And their love flows into us. That is burden-bearing.

✳ A good night, but a short one. We rose early to get to the hospital by nine o'clock for our consult with Liz. Before we left, Harold had a fall on the stairs, not stumbling so much as snagging his rubber-soled shoes on the carpeting. He caught himself on the handrail and it swung him around sharply. No damage done, but he felt the pull in his scarred left side and shoulder. Now, when his side hurts, we'll ask, Is it from surgery and scar tissue, or this fall, or cancer? The cancer question is always waiting there, crouched behind every ache or weakness.

Liz gave us a half an hour and described two new spots that had shown up on the most recent bone scan. None of the others has diminished in size or intensity. She went on to tell us of the chemotherapy options: "Standard treatment" uses a combination of anti-cancer agents and is administered either by injections and pills on an outpatient basis, or to an inpatient receiving the drugs intravenously once a month. The other option is the use of an experimental or "investigative" drug which, it is hoped, will have fewer undesirable side effects. The effectiveness rate for the first option is twenty-five to thirty percent. For the second, the effectiveness rate is unknown, a question mark.

Typically, this is a galloping cancer. That Harold is as well as he is, and that he is ambulatory, still active, and working, is, Liz feels, an answer to prayer. My immediate, interior response: If God is going to answer prayer to that extent, why not heal my husband completely? What good is it merely to slow the progress of the disease? We're buying time, but what for? All that chemotherapy offers is, maybe fifty or sixty more days of life.

Every day is a gift, of course, precious and worthwhile. But it's shocking to talk about a few more days of life when our families—both sides—are characterized by longevity.

Liz wants Harold to go on the outpatient chemo—that is, to start *today* on a regimen of Cytoxan, Adriamycin, Methotrexate, and Procarbazine hydrochloride. They call it CAMP for short. The first three are injections. The Procarbazine is taken daily in pills.

Later. It was really a boost to learn that the CAT scan of the soft tissues is clear. Liver, kidneys, pancreas, adrenals—all look healthy, and the mediastinal lymph nodes and two glitches in the right lung have shown no change since the scan back in September. It could be the bark tea. Or prayer. Or both.

After our office visit with Dr. Hillman, we were shown into the "chemotherapy suite." A nurse-technician administered the three drugs given intravenously, with saline solution flowing in before, between, and after. She also gave us literature on chemo, an explanation of the possible side effects of each drug, and a phone number if we have questions. We are to call if Harold has fever or any unusual bleeding. To help him tolerate the effects of the chemo drugs, he can have Compazine (anti-nausea), and Vistaril (an antihistamine).

It was 7:00 P.M. when we left. The clinic parking lot was empty, and the wind was swirling tongues of snow around my feet as I went out to get the car and fetch Harold from the ER entrance. Strange how the decision about chemotherapy seems to have been made for us.

Saturday morning the Group arrived here for brunch. Harold surprised me by waking from his drugged sleep, showering, and joining the rest of us for the meal, in good spirits. I distributed Bibles, paper, and pencils and assigned each person three or four verses from Hebrews 12, allowing each fifteen minutes to study and paraphrase it in his or her own words, as if expressing the ideas to a younger person. I was amazed how well the paraphrases worked. As we read through the whole chapter in sequence, the insights were extraordinary.

After the others had left, Karen, Marlene, and Jack stayed to pray for Harold. As I explained to them, I am aghast at what we are doing with the chemotherapy—deliberately introducing strong poisons into Harold's body. We all prayed that God would transform this "bad" into good.

✱ Because of the weather we stayed home Sunday. Jeff is here from NYC, sick and feverish. Kris has a juicy cold. These infections make me very nervous for H. who is supposed to be protected from infectious disease. He struggled all night with nausea, taking three Compazine, which left him like a zombie Monday. Worse, he has lost all appetite. Yesterday all he could do was lie down or pace slowly back and forth like an old and weary lion in a cage.

I'm scared. We have traded Harold's relative well-being and comfort for this sub-existence, and a body full of destructive poison. When I came to bed last night I too felt pretty desperate, and shed some hot tears. H. saw them, and I think it snapped him out of his withdrawal because he hugged me and prayed for me, "Lord, please comfort and strengthen Lu." I have had no time or peace myself to read and pray lately; broken nights and fragmented days have left me ragged.

✳ Harold, Jeff, and I spent a good hour today discussing the future of HSP (Harold Shaw Publishers). Two possibilities: Sell out to another publisher, or retain ownership and employ a manager. We are concerned about if and where Jeff should be involved. He appreciates being wanted, and knows it would have to be more than just a business; it is a ministry. While he respects our books and what we are doing, he must wait until his own faith and life are more stable.

As I see through Jeff's eyes, I find my own thinking drifting in a skeptical direction. In the past I have had cycles of uncertainty, attacks of agnosticism, and have struggled with the questions, "Can anyone really know anything beyond a shadow of doubt?" Yet again and again I have been encouraged in books and sermons and my own thinking to "Hang in there," "Be patient, and persist," "Choose to believe." From *The Cloud of Unknowing:* "Smite upon the thick cloud of unknowing with a sharp dart of longing love; come what may, do not give up." January 1, just over a year ago, I made a vow in the presence of the Mains and the Bosches never to desert the faith.

And now I am being rigorously tested.

✳ Kris is in the middle of finals, Jeff is coming home late at night and sleeping in, Harold is catnapping at odd hours. This means I have to prepare a lot of single, odd meals throughout the day and the kitchen is always a mess, either from food being prepared or from the chaos afterwards. Things are never *finished.* Shoes, books, papers, pillows, glasses, and dishes are strewn about and I feel frustration about the disorder. I don't nag—simply live the life of a picker-upper—but it bothers me that no one else seems to notice.

Tuesday afternoon I took Harold out in the car for a fresh perspective after his housebound days. We stopped at the office to approve a new book jacket design for David Watson's *Fear*

No Evil. The publishing goes on inexorably. I try to write back cover copy for *Five Evangelical Leaders* and end up editing Randy's copy for the rest of the catalog. It's the constant pull between home and office duties that leaves me feeling guilty about the one I'm not doing at any given moment!

Evidently Jeff has set some kind of record for the shortest training period prior to getting his seat on the Exchange—four months. He is reading my copy of *The Dancing Wu Li Masters,* and I also gave him Virginia Stem Owens' *And the Trees Clap Their Hands* for a Christian view of the new physics. I think Jeff is looking, as I am, for some explanation of reality that includes both the insights of modern science and the teaching of Christianity—some "unified field theory" that sits well, meshes with orthodox theology.

✱ Now we're at the outpatient clinic again, where H. is having x-rays and blood work done before our appointment with Liz Hillman. The nurses here in hematology/oncology say, "Oh, you'll get to know all of us pretty soon!" Today Joanne was our nurse but Jeanne, who administered the IV last week, also dropped in to see us. It's nice of them to be so friendly, but we don't *want* to get too well-acquainted with this place, these kind people, the all-pervasive ambience of cancer.

Harold's IV chemotherapy went much more easily this time—one vein did it for all three drugs—the clear, colorless Cytoxan, the wine red Adriamycin, the sulphur yellow Methotrexate. We left the hospital after three o'clock, with an appointment for blood tests next week at the clinic.

With all four drugs in him at once, H. began to feel queasy. The nausea continued all night, complicated by Kris's constant cough—a deep bark which sounded ominous.

✳ Lunch with Don and Edie Tinder, who plan to go to Europe and teach at a new seminary. Don asked about our move from Bethany Chapel to St. Mark's and seemed incredulous that after generations of family history in the Plymouth Brethren, and Harold's being an *elder,* we could "throw over our heritage." To someone who is quite satisfied with the system, it was hard for us to explain our need for a different way of looking at life and faith. But I think about it a lot. The Episcopal way of worship—with its show and tell, its sacramental interpretation of life, its richness of sign and symbol—speaks to my imagination and awakens a fresh, inner response. At first it was just one unexpected epiphany after another, but now it has become second nature—the vocal responses, the easy movement from knees to pew to standing to altar, the Peace, the genuflection, and the crossing of oneself to signal the inner blessings of grace from Father, Son, and Spirit. At first, I rebelled at incense. Now the pungent aroma triggers my sense of smell which instantly speaks to my spirit—"prayer rising to God." I love the progression from the Liturgy of the Word, with its tying together of Scripture from Old and New Testaments, the Psalms, the Gospels, to the Liturgy of the Table with the bread and wine pressing a tender consciousness of Christ's enfleshment into my heart. These moments in the intimacy of the body of Christ are what hold me in faith. They call me to mystery and Godhead.

After the Tinders left, I took Kris to the clinic where the doctor diagnosed bronchitis—and sent her home with erythromycin and cough medicine. Later, when she went to bed and I had rubbed her down with lotion and dosed her up with medication and plugged in the vaporizer and applied Vicks and flannel to her chest and prayed with her, she looked up at me and said, "Mom, thank you so *much*." That makes any work worthwhile.

✳ Right after my conversation with Jeff about the new physics, *Christianity Today* arrived in the mail with two articles on that very subject. Contrary to the fears of some conservative theologians, so these writers argue, theories of quantum physics may well be consonant with the reality of God. The problem is a semantic one. We lack language and imagery by which to describe and understand both God and the behavior of sub-atomic particles. Living with a husband with cancer, I find my thoughts struggling with providence and its directions, trying to join them with the random vectors of science. Yet if we have one God, Creator of all, it must fit; it must cohere.

✳ Sunday I went to church after trying and failing to feed H. the poached egg I cooked him. Nausea took over and nudged me out of the way. Kris is still fevered and coughing. I left them at 8:45 and felt the strong and settling impact of the liturgy. Rick preached from the Old Testament reading in Jeremiah 3—the Israelites worshiping pagan gods on the high places—turning away from the truth to the counterfeit. I felt a tug inside. Is that what I am doing—moving away from orthodox belief with my questioning? I want truth, reality. *If God is real, I'm moving in his direction, not away from him.* In the service I reaffirmed my resolve never to abandon God, but to persist in seeking him, waiting for him to show himself to me.

On the way to the St. Mark's parish meeting with Karen that evening, I shared some of my frustrations—Harold's grumpiness, my inability to find food that pleases him, Kris's illness, my own emotional fatigue, also my interest in the new physics realm. She wants to read up on it. At least she won't think I'm apostate with my metaphysical but intensely urgent questions.

I'm coughing deeply again, with sinus pain. Monday I was panicky enough about my deep, booming cough to see my friend Susan Cole, an internist at the Wheaton Medical Clinic.

Yes, definite congestion in the left lung. Take erythromycin and a cough suppressant.

Kris is still in bed. Harold is weaker and more nauseated than I've yet seen him, barely moving around at all. He refuses all food.

Karen brought over some cheese soup for our supper and cleaned up my messy kitchen. It wasn't until she left, and I was sorting some of the paper that constantly flows in through the mail, that I picked up my billing from the clinic and noticed the diagnosis Sue Cole had written on it—"Early pneumonia."

With Harold running a slight fever, my fear, of course, is that he'll contract either Kris's bronchitis or my pneumonia, since chemotherapy lowers white blood cell and platelet counts which provide protection against infection.

Having Harold and me both sick is very hard on Kris. She must feel so unprotected, though others are pitching in to help. Yesterday she threw herself on my bed and wailed, "Oh Mom, when are you going to get better?" I think today she's angry. I want to tell her it's all right to be angry, not at God, but as David Alexander put it, at this whole rotten, fallen creation with its disease and death, angry at the Satan behind it all.

Now, it seems, I have pleurisy, and can't sleep for the pain. In bed I read Kay Lindskoog's *A Gift of Dreams*. Beyond the unconscious mind it also seems as though someone, or something external to the dreamer, is orchestrating the whole process.

I seldom recall dreams, but there is one persistent image I have had all my life—so strong and real in my mind that it seems more historic than dreamlike. What I see is an extension to our house, huge wings of unexplored, unlived-in rooms gorgeously furnished, full of fascinating *objets d'art*, that seem to wait to be used, but never are. I want entry to that richness.

Two

Jack and Meg D'Arcy have offered us the use of their Sanibel condominium. Liz Hillman gave her OK to Harold's going, provided he gets plenty of rest, gentle exercise, and not too much sun. The dean at Kris's school thinks she should go with us.

I can see it in my mind, hardly believing it—sand, sea, sky, shells, but no snow. Blissful contrast—there's a foot of snow here and the temperature hovers around zero. (Both cars died with the cold again, even in the garage.)

* South in the sun, the condo, decorated in pale Florida colors, is elegant and comfortable and overlooks the flour-white beach. It is like Paradise to be here. Each day follows the last with a bright froth curling off its crest, like waves in sequence, the air flowing in from the Gulf, carrying glistening particles of salt, sand, and spray.

Standing here on the beach, we find ourselves at the joining of elements—earth, air, water (and the sun adds a fourth—

fire). The distances are tremendous; a whole continent stretches itself horizontally away behind us, as does the sea in front of us; the ocean floor plummets from the continental shelf to an invisible depth at our feet, dark blue and mysterious; and the sky without clouds—we can look up and up forever through its light-years of distance. All these infinities meet and mark us, and dance with each other, on this very spot. The edges shift in and out a bit with winds and tides, but these fundamental borders give us a sense of the universe and the acts of God.

I am amazed at how effortlessly I slip into a beachcomber role. As I pad along the shore, eyes scanning the millions of shells in their textured banks, or scattered, embedded in the film of the pulled-back waves, my mind keeps saying to me, *This is pure happiness. This is the state of purest happiness.*

Bright bits of color catch me in the eye—rosy, rubbery seaweed, a pearly jingle shell, a ribbed calico cockle patterned in bright tangerine, a live sea-star, a glistening angel-wing— undeserved gifts of Grace winking up at me with the sheen of sun and sea on them, waiting to be fondled with the eye or carried away with me a thousand miles to where they can remind me of these perfect moments. As I bend and lift each one and love it with my touch and glance, I wonder if this was how God bent and lifted me, how he chose me and treasures me, how he wants me with him. I must seem singular and precious to him if he came so far to find me.

✱ Harold's hair is falling out now—a fine rain of fiber. Every morning on the pillow, I see the strange gleaning from the night's tossings and turnings. He looks vulnerable and naked. He feels it, too—an external but drastic change in the way he sees himself.

Today, with the wind at fifty knots and the rain driving in, the force of the weather is healing, elemental. Huge breakers endlessly crash against the shoreline, throwing up a salt mist, churning the thick layers of shells and making a clinking rustle as the brine sucks down and away through them. After coffee, Harold and I walk the shore with the wind literally pushing us forward, irresistible as the Spirit. Clouds scud close over us at an oblique angle with the sun suddenly breaking through to water the sea's rough silk with milky light. A rim of rain obscures the horizon. All the gulls, terns, plovers, and sanderlings are standing, cowed-looking, on the shore, heads away from the gusts, tail feathers ruffled, waiting for the wind to die.

Last night after dinner a brilliant sunset poured between the clouds like melted gold. I ran down to the beach to catch it on film before the fire died. There's a splendid satisfaction in having a record of the weather in its several moods. I can recall it, courtesy of my slides and my journal, and in some future moment the visual impression calls up the other sense impressions—the tang of the spray driven by the singing air, the buffet of wind on cheekbone, the crunch of shells underfoot, the unceasing sounds of the sea.

J. B. Phillips says that the ocean is irresistibly attractive because it reminds us of eternity. I'd put infinite space in there too, as a link between the sea and the eternal state. The endless in-wrinkling of waves is one clue, the unknown depth another. The waves' continuous arrival shows me an ongoing diversity which is never monotonous because an infinite innovation lies behind it. Each arc of water up the beach, each configuration of shells and stones and dunes and grasses is unique, unrepeatable.

✳ In the aftermath of the storm comes its harvest. The waves and their deep turbulence have knocked loose and laid at our feet shells not seen in the earlier, calmer days of this week. Today I have found apple murex, turbans, zebra nerites, distorsios, jewel boxes, tellins, coquinas, spiny oysters, tulips, turnip whelks, moon snails, babies' ears, many of them alive, that is with their original inhabitants still attached and lively (though in one helmet I found a squatter—a hermit crab which appeared and disappeared quick as a blink).

I find that I cannot choose shells for others, nor they for me. The oiled and varnished specimens in all the gift shops hold no attraction for me. Sometimes, walking the beach, Harold or Kris will pick up a shell to give me, but by their choosing it they have already made it theirs. To me, shells are a parable of personal choice and significance. A volute or a junonia is fascinating in itself—"a folding-out of pink and white, a letting-in of spiral light,"—but the incident of noticing it in its own setting and taking it for my own renders it notable; its selection is part of its history. Mentally, I see any treasured shell in its original company—an aggregate of shapes and sizes in melon, chestnut, dappled mauve, dawn yellow, dusk, or taupe. We each search out our own best colors, our favorite shapes.

✱ This week I've been reading Walker Percy's *The Second Coming* whose central figure, Will Barrett, is agnostic but trying to find a place to stand between unbelief and what Percy views as the cloying kind of fundamentalism prevalent in the south. I can hardly wait to find out how the book ends.

✱ Home again. I asked the Lord during the Eucharist at St. Mark's this morning to transcend my unknowing and minister his grace to me, even if I am too numb to feel it. More—while I consumed the wafer and wine, the holy solid and fluid that speak of Christ's body and which I accept as his gifts to me—I offered myself and all my unknowing as an exchange gift to him.

✱ Harold has gone one better than Samson. He has lost his hair and regained his strength! I am thinking that it's time to reassess his physical progress which happens so subtly and slyly that we don't notice it unless we deliberately compare *now* with a point in past time, say six weeks ago. Apart from some breathlessness after exertion (he shoveled snow away from the mailbox after lunch—something he could never have attempted last month), he is symptom-free. The pain in his leg has almost disappeared. He looks less gaunt, has regained some weight, can lie comfortably on either right or left side at night for a couple of hours, is hardly moaning, groaning, or grunting at all. We see Dr. Hillman Friday. And Sue Cole thinks my pneumonia has resolved after two courses of antibiotics, though some of the pleurisy pain is still with me, jabbing me when I move suddenly.

✱ The pile of mail we returned to seems mountainous—my delight which has become my urgent burden. My heart rushes to answer every letter I open, but there is no time to write down the words. Our HSP quarterly planning meeting took up one whole day here at home, which meant planning lunch for eight as well as giving devotions. In the editorial meeting it was decided to publish my newest poems under the title *Postcard from the Shore* this fall, which means I will have to polish about twenty unfinished poems in the next few months, find a cover photo, write a foreword, and ask critics to write endorsements.

✱ We face a new appointment with Liz Hillman, and H. and I have both been anxious about what she will suggest next. Neither of us has positive reactions to going through another devastating chemotherapy cycle. Separately and together we have been thinking of refusing the chemo. This is very tricky. Who are we to make such a decision in the face of skilled medical advice? On what basis do we opt out of the system? Yet it is Harold's body and our lives that bear the brunt of either cancer or chemo. The choice seems impossible; chemo may lengthen his life a month, but at the cost of such weakness and misery that that month seems not worth living. Yet if we skip it, and let this transient period of well-being continue uninterrupted, will we look back later and regret that we didn't do everything humanly possible?

✱ A minor but continued frustration—the Peugeot battery and electrical system. H. took it to LaGrange for testing and repair—spending over $150 and five hours, and on the way home the heater still wasn't working right.

✱ I have finished *The Second Coming*. After Will Barrett and Allie have found each other—"His heart leapt with a secret joy. What is it I want from her and him (the old priest), he wondered, not only want but must have? Is she a gift and therefore a sign of a giver? Could it be that the Lord is here, masquerading behind this silly simple holy face? Am I crazy to want both, her and Him? No, not want, must have, and will have." The name Will Barrett speaks to me about the importance of the will in such things. "Will have" means "chooses to have" and never relinquishing the choice.

✳ In the doctor's office there's a striking poster—a photo of the Grand Canyon, all purple and bronze, curves and contrasts of clefts and strata down to the deep mystery of the canyon bottom. We have stood at the actual place where the photograph was taken. Such a poster redeems the sterile square blankness of the examining room. Its title—"Time and the River Flowing." The huge magnificence of the Grand Canyon somehow moves into the constricted space with its orange plastic chairs.

Liz seems more relaxed than usual, pleased with Harold's vigor, with the fact that he hasn't lost weight, with his nice tan. She understands how he feels about the chemo but argues for not abandoning the program after only one cycle.

Harold looks at me. What are we to say? Shall we stick with our feelings and insist *No more chemo*? I feel torn, dreading the effects of the drugs on H.'s body, mind, and spirit. "It's too soon to judge the effectiveness of the treatment. There are probably cancer cells that are beginning to be knocked out," she persists, "and we need more chemo to continue the process." Continue? But would it really finish them off? We give in, bowing to her expertise. Why see an oncologist if you don't take the advice given?

When H. is under chemotherapy (*under* is the right word— it's like being covered with a damp tarpaulin), I feel so cut off from him. He says that chemo makes him feel lonely inside himself too, strange and estranged. I can tell he's beginning to recover from the chemo when he returns my kiss or hug instead of remaining inert. He often gives a little grunt that can mean either approval or distress; sometimes I can't tell which.

✳ I am rereading Walker Percy's *The Second Coming*. Repelled by mass-produced, prepackaged Christian belief and the black despair and futility of his own agnosticism, Will seeks a signal from God. He enters the cave under the mountain to wait for a resolution—a yes, a no—from God. Interrupted in this vigil by that most mundane of all exigencies—a toothache—he scrabbles his way out through subterranean passages, lost in the dark, bleeding, struggling, "feeling the whole weight of the mountain on his chest," to burst (as from a womb), into the greenhouse with its warmth and light and fertility and verdure—a most lovely metaphor for rebirth.

For him, the second coming of Christ was heralded by the advent, the influx into his life of new love and hope in the person of Allie, a little crazy, speaking (almost) another language. The story is so plangent—it resounds in my echo chamber mind. It shows me what the advent of Christ *feels like*.

✱ In today's Lenten service fasting was mentioned—a theme which has been glancing off the top of my mind like a skipped stone, but which now begins to sink deeper. At coffee hour I talked to Karen about it and about the problem the family cook has in fasting (which essentially means taking time from meal preparation and eating to focus on God instead) while having to prepare three meals a day for the family. My mind is constantly preoccupied with food, because I need to think of new ways of getting nourishment into H., with him resisting every step of the way!

Karen and I have decided to skip one meal a day, to be accountable to each other, and to attend Communion at least once during the week. Perhaps this will help me to focus on things of the Spirit, since I've had no time for reflection and prayer, little concentration on deeper realities. Our mealtime prayers seem perfunctory. I feel perfunctory. I feel I'm fulfilling everyone's demands but God's.

✱ Listening to the tapes of the King's College Choir singing Bach's: "Death, death, I will not fear thee, though thou standest near me. Grave, grave, I calmly spurn thee, though to dust thou turn me, strong in hope and faith." The words in their music felt like a core of light flooding to my extremities. Then, the chanting of the Nicene creed all on one pure, sustained, almost disembodied note. The psalms in Anglican chant—music that is pure delight on both the visceral and mental levels because the music and words are channeled in structure that informs both mind and soul.

✱ The homily on Sunday was about Peter's affirmation of Christ as God. Part of me gladly makes that same affirmation. Another part of me hesitates and holds back. I thought of the cloud which covered Jesus and the disciples during the Transfiguration—a "cloud of unknowing" which blocked Jesus from their sight. It seems that if we are disciples who want to be close to Jesus, as the three were, we must go through that cloud, or wait for it to lift and the Father to reveal the Son to us. Meanwhile, we live in the blinding mist on our way up the mountain.

Three

Because of the ice storm earlier this week the power is out all over town. Scanning the poems in *A Widening Light,* I chanced on Chad Walsh's poem, "Why has thou forsaken me?" and heard the words from Psalm 22 echoing my frequent feelings:

> I have called to God and heard no answer,
> I have seen the thick curtain drop and sunlight
>   die;
> My voice has echoed back, a foolish voice,
> The prayer restored intact
> to its silly source.
> I have walked in darkness, he hung in it.
> In all my mines of night, he was there first;
> In whatever dead tunnel I am lost, he finds me.
> My God, my God, why has thou forsaken me?
> From his perfect darkness a voice says, "I have
>   not."

How can darkness be perfect? When it is part of God's purpose. Perhaps he planned this darkness, this power outage, as a demonstration for me, just as he planned it for his Son, so that the darkness may be banished when the power comes back. This way we see darkness for what it is—absence of light. It seemed a word of the Lord to me in the moment I read it. I can't see him—the darkness is too thick. All I want is a touch—hand, shoulder, robe—so that I know he is with me in this place until the lights come on and my eyes squint for the glory of it.

✱ Rick's sermon today, on the feeding of the five thousand, asked us to identify ourselves either with Philip, absorbed with counting the costs of the catering, or Andrew, who found some inadequate food supplies but brought them, with faith, to the Lord; he included the Lord in his equation. Rick suggested that we each think of a desirable yet impossible thing and see it as possible through God's power. His message pierced me. I know the two things I want to ask. I have been Philip; I want to be Andrew. And I want my husband well.

✱ Kristin has been critical of me recently, no matter how hard I strive to be diplomatic, thoughtful, understanding, and loving, though she is very lovingly demonstrative with Harold. Today, after listening to a taped talk on "unfailing love," it occurred to me that God may be showing me, a parent, what he feels when I, his child, fail to believe, trust, and love him. In my own experience of rejection, I can feel his sadness.

Psalm 109:4 expresses my resolve concerning Kris: "Despite my love, they accuse me; but as for me, I will pray for them." I am sensing David's hurt and anger in the Psalms, his human condition, his need; I am in there with him. We join hands over millennia. The emotions in his words resonate with my own, jumping the huge temporal and geographical gap.

✱ Harold was up at dawn yesterday for an LBI Board meeting. The pace quickens. He is cramming more and more into his days.

Randy and Vange had come to me the evening before, concerned about company morale. The staff feel the uncertainty about the future for HSP, as well as for us personally. I tried to reassure them today that we contemplate no major company changes. Harold seems to be caught up in the swing of leadership, but he is putting off a decision about finding someone to manage the company. I feel we should begin some investigating, now. We had a vigorous argument.

I heard H. talking on a transatlantic call this morning. "Yes, my prognosis is excellent and that encourages us a lot." That's certainly not how I'd put it. And I know Dr. Hillman wouldn't. Death stalks us. Is Harold putting up a barrier of denial? Does he believe he's healed?

✱ We're at the clinic in the Internal Medicine subspecialties section waiting for chemotherapy. Yesterday was a glory, full of Bach music—his three hundredth birthday being celebrated on TV and radio. On the drive in, more Bach—"If Thou be with me," his song written to his young wife, Anna Magdalena, about the imminence of death, which seems strange coming from a thirty-seven-year-old man. But life then was much shorter and even more perilous than now.

Liz wants H. to go through two more chemo cycles, and then evaluate. She's encouraged that the leg pain is gone, that his weight is unchanged, and that he's working full days. But even if the evaluation shows no spread of cancer, she wants to continue with the chemo. (*How long, O Lord?*) If the chemo is ineffective (i.e., if the cancer spreads), she'll stop the treatment. Two appalling alternatives.

✱ I talked with a friend about Kris's attitude. Though painful for me, it is probably healthy, she thinks. Kris can't attack Harold, but she has to vent her hurt and anger, and I'm available. Seeing it like that, I realize I can stand it.

✱ At our Group meeting David led us in several rounds of prayer based on such questions as: "What is your highest priority from Christ for the coming week?" or "What is your vision for the future of St. Mark's?" and ending with "What do you need God to be for you?" My prayers were for spiritual vitality and for the Father to be like the sun licking away the cloud of unknowing with its heat, and piercing my heart, filling my veins with fire.

Later, David talked about the prayer of acceptance, before going to bed, which releases our tensions and gives any situation into God's hands.

I do that now, Lord. I give you my concern about Jeff and Kris. I give you Harold's "gray" mood and manner following his chemo. I accept their reality and pray that in your time you'll make things different.

Sunday, the service peaked for me twice; in Communion when I felt that link with God in the receiving and mouthing of the bread, and the touch of the chalice's edge, and the sting of wine on my lips—the bridge stepped on, the connection made. Then again, in the singing of hymn 446, whose last stanza goes:

> Hope on then, broken spirit,
> Hope on, be not afraid.
> Fear not the griefs that plague thee
> And keep thy heart dismayed.
> Thy God in his great mercy
> Will save thee, hold thee fast,

And in his own time grant thee
The sun of joy at last.

Harold seems better with each day, once again thinking strongly of canceling further chemo treatment so that we can make the most of the good days he has left. We waffle between hope and resignation, but live the good days as if each is all we have.

✳ Sunday. At 6:30 I left for St. Mark's and the Great Vigil of Easter. As I drove the twelve miles to Geneva, I tried to identify just what it is I am missing spiritually—what I want of God. I think I lack a sense of exhilaration and excitement about him—which may be what joy is. During the readings of the service, I was struck with words from Ezekiel about God giving his people a heart of flesh instead of a heart of stone. *Lord, please melt, or break, my stony heart.*

I was scheduled to read from Romans 5. Got cassocked and surpliced with the other readers and we received large candles. The whole church was plunged into darkness and a fire was ignited in a brazier, which filled the space with flickering light blazing up in the shadows. Each of our candles was lit from the burning charcoal, and we in turn passed the flame to the smaller candles held by the people in the congregation, so that the sanctuary was pricked with scores of lights. I love the way the Episcopal church shows as well as tells the truth. My mind, my senses are engaged by it all; why are my heart responses often caught in neutral?

✳ Though Harold is increasingly active, he has been depressed. The business pressures build as he resumes his normal role and work load. I hate to see him growing tense and edgy again.

I, too, am mentally and physically fatigued, and the press of detail is on me. The house needs cleaning and organizing; stacks of letters wait to be answered. H. is working on taxes, which he's trying to instruct me about (it's like trying to introduce a hen to metaphysics). The daily snow showers are depressing. I yearn for warmth and freedom to read and think and feed my spirit.

✶ Gentle rain today, but warmer, and green—*green*!

Rick preached on a phrase from the Collect: "Grant that all who have been reborn into the fellowship of Christ's Body may show forth in their lives what they profess by their faith." It was a message for "professional Christians," those who know it all, yet whose testimony has expired from lack of reality. Rick emphasized the radical nature of the new birth transformation and why it is not existentially active in so many of us. I felt my heart quicken. He was speaking to me! He used the vision of the Wadi of Dry Bones, needing not only flesh and skin to cover them (the true teachings of the gospel) but breath to fill them, to activate the mechanism (the moving Spirit). I thought, again, of Ezekiel 11:19: "I will ... put a new spirit within them, and I will take the stony heart out of their flesh and give them a heart of flesh." The paradoxical people—body of flesh, heart of stone—God wants to integrate, to unify by the Spirit's power until they are *alive clear through,* the cold, dead, hard core replaced by a warm pulsing heart that is a part of the rest of their flesh.

My prayer: *Transfuse me, re-oxygenate my spirit. By the electricity of your life in me, you have been nudging me across the frontier. My faith has not been one grand leap, but a series of small, halting steps toward you. It's like a dance between us; I wanted You to do the work, the revelation, but passive waiting was not enough to get the dancing going. I must step out on the floor and trust you to step toward me.*

✱ This is one of the beautiful days of the year, warm, with every branch carrying a lace of early green, or at least a family of swollen buds.

The sun shining through the unfolding, pale green leaves highlights them against the dark trunks and fence posts. Pure spring. In one of Emily Dickinson's letters there is the phrase—"the lawn is filled with south." This is such a morning. In celebration, I just wrote a Dickinsonian stanza:

> The air is filled with south—
> Breath which though soft, unseen,
> Pants warm from some far, tropic mouth
> And mists the world with green.

The record-breaking heat continues, forcing even the stubborn oaks to burst and bud. Today is a spring work day— spraying for dandelions, cutting grass, raking, fertilizing—all the good things we do, with enthusiasm at first, which become onerous duties later in the summer. I see parallels with the initial joy of conversion and the creeping staleness that so often seems to flatten out the zeal profile of older Christians.

✱ Harold is shaky and weak. Yesterday's yard work was too much for him, though I made him rest often. I can see he is worried about it. After dinner he seemed sunk in lethargy, unable to talk. He looks a bit ghostly and is stooped, though he has lost no weight and feels no pain. We are making a consistent effort to walk at least a mile every day, but having one lung limits him.

Late in the day we call Liz Hillman, who seems reluctant to discuss the results of Harold's most recent tests over the phone but admits that no new cancer has shown up, and that possibly there is "some improvement," though the CEA reading has not come back yet. I think she was afraid if the news was good, we might not bother to see her Friday. H. and I are both feeling a gentle, warm relief.

✳ I've been lying in bed for an hour, my mind so full of piercing thought that I am forced to write. I have been blown up like a balloon with realities like dying and pain and freedom and tears, and conflicts like the arrival of spring and the imminence of decay and death. I am under the gun to complete the Foreword to *Postcard* . . . and polish the twenty new poems that are still in rough draft. That kind of pressure is like forcing fruit or blossoms in a conservatory, rather than allowing them to ripen and open and flush with color in their own time, with the seasons, and periods of dormancy and growth. I'm afraid of printing poems before they can prove their maturity.

✳ Friday we drive down to see Dr. Hillman. In the examining room Liz has set up the three sets of bone scans for us to view, and points out the similarities between them, and the fact that this last scan shows no new hot spots. The shock comes, though, when she reports that the CEA, the tumor marker test, now reads 280. Last December it was 70. This tells us that in spite of Harold's lack of pain, his stabilized weight and overall feeling of well-being, an active tumor is growing somewhere in his body.

The burning question is whether to continue the chemo. "It has to be Harold's decision," I say, "He's the one who has to live through it." Liz nods her head in agreement. Her final recommendation: H. should go through one more chemo cycle, and then re-test the CEA to see if it goes up or down. If it is up, we'll stop.

I couldn't help it. Sitting in the corner, on the little shelf seat beside the changing room curtain, I leaned my head against the wall with the tears running down my face. Harold sat there, wordless. Hope is such a fragile feeling. Like the Holy Ghost, it is easily quenched.

Spring is a promise
in the closed fist
of a long winter. All
we have is a raw
slant of light at a low
angle, a rising river
of wind, and an icy rain
that drowns out green
in a tide of mud. It is
the daily postponement
that disillusions.
(Once again the performance
has been canceled by
the management.) We live
on legends of old
springs. Each evening
brings only remote
possibilities of
renewal: "Maybe
tomorrow." But the

evening and the morning
are the umpteenth day
and the God of sunlit
Eden still looks
on the weather
and calls it good.

III

THE FACE
IN THE CLOUD

May–October 1985

*We search for a self to be. There is still
something crucial missing . . . we search
for that unfound thing too.*

—FREDERICK BUECHNER, **The Sacred Journey**

One

May Day. I spent an early hour outside in the garden planting pachysandra and a little mugho pine, good and deep and wet. With cancer in the house I feel the need to promote healthy growth and new life.

✱ Harold's hair is beginning to grow back—a fine fuzz that's pale but unmistakable. Kris and I trimmed off more of the three-inch-long wisps that were left of the old growth, and the effect is that of a very short crewcut.

He called Liz Hillman just now to tell her of his decision to cancel further chemo, a decision reached through prayer this week. She reluctantly agreed even though his CEA hasn't been retested since the 280 reading of April 26. She asked that he "keep in touch." I know she cares about him, as a patient, as a person. Next appointment, May 31.

So that is that—chemo *over*. Medical resources exhausted, back to dependence on the body's immune systems, and prayer. We feel free and exhilarated.

Shortly after that conversation, it started to sprinkle and has rained steadily all afternoon and evening, though it is warm and doesn't seem to matter. In fact, I have a sense of satisfaction, knowing my annuals and perennials are planted. I can feel them enjoying the rain and getting established as their roots work down into the wet soil.

✳ Harold has been reading *Christ the Healer* and his spirits seem as buoyant and confident as I have seen them in months. It doesn't surprise me that his physical state varies according to his state of mind. In his days of faith, with no solid *physical* evidence to go on, he believes he is being healed. But when he feels pain in his leg or chest, or has indigestion, his confidence is dampened. He doesn't want to discourage me either, but even if he doesn't voice the complaints, his whole demeanor betrays what he is feeling.

Tonight I went to hear Walt Wangerin speak on the power of suffering. As I listened a strong impulse moved up inside me and welled into tears. I wonder if I have been steeling myself against emotion, afraid of letting go and losing control in the recent effort to overcome doubts and fears about death. In my mind I have accused Harold of denial. I may be guilty of it myself.

✳ When Bob and Bobbie Kuhne arrived to pray tonight, H. read to them from Psalm 116:

> I love the Lord because he hears my prayers and answers them. Because he bends down and listens, I will pray as long as I breathe!

Death stared me in the face—I was frightened and sad.

Then I cried 'Lord, save me!'

How kind he is! How good he is!

So merciful, this God of ours!

The Lord protects the simple and childlike; I was facing death and then he saved me.

Now I can relax. For the Lord has done this wonderful miracle for me.

He has saved me from death, my eyes from tears, my feet from stumbling.

I shall live! Yes, in his presence—here on earth!

But now, what can I offer Jehovah for all he has done for me? . . .

His loved ones are very precious to him, and he does not lightly let them die (vv. 1–9, 12, 15 TLB).

The passage seems written just for us and our needs. It is hard for me, though, to be "simple and childlike" with the intuitive trust of a young child rather than the sort of seasoned skepticism I find in myself. *Lord, give me a child's heart.*

✳ Yesterday, in a Mother's Day card, a letter came from Jeff. It was more than a conventional greeting; it was full of the Jeff we love to see—thanking me for letters, love, and concern for his life direction. Telling of depression at the theft of his new motorcycle. Mentioning the possibility of moving back to Chicago now that NYC has bred in him a new independence and self-confidence. Telling of the fear of committal to Christianity because while at Wheaton, "trying hard to be a strong Christian," he had been so miserable. He wrote: "I guess my difficulty at this point doesn't stem from unbelief or a hard heart. I want to believe . . . but I'm afraid to re-embrace those ideals again and then fail. If I fail, I might be left with very little to believe in at all." He ended with "Thanks again for being a wonderful mother. All my love. Jeff."

✱ Because of the increasingly warm weather we have put in some of the window screens and removed storm windows. I noticed Harold giving me careful instructions "This side faces out. *This* end is at the top." And each day continues the instructional litany "This is how you set the timer on the water softener." "Let me show you the things to watch in this bank statement." "This is the proportion of oil to gasoline for the riding mower." He's hedging his bets, looking on both the bright side and the dark side, telling me how to cope without him—in case I have to.

✱ With the Bosches for prayer, as so often happens, it was as if an electrical current ran between us, engendering confidence that God is at work. H. has been discouraged when doctors such as John and Wendell Searer talk about remission rather than healing. It's a delicate balance to keep. I too want him to face realities, but not to lose all hope.

Driving home, the sky was so freshly clear and purely blue, with greens of enamel and emeralds—a strange intensity, like the universe singing and vibrating with life. We are a part of it, and we don't want to fade out of it.

Yet, paradoxically, I have been losing the sense of faith restored. I think I know how it happens. The joy of it seems to produce a contentment that slides into complacency, so that the cutting edge of desire is blunted.

There are only two alternatives—I can either change my ways and plan time to seek God's face, to focus, to reach for him, or I can fill all my time with other urgencies, lose touch with him, and slip back into my discontent and blunted belief. He's asking me, "What do you really want? Decide, and do it." But this has been a lifelong struggle, and it is not likely to be resolved so easily.

* I have sent off all my unpublished poems, about fifteen of them, to different magazines. Also finished off my evaluation of portions of the NIV Study Bible. Yesterday I wrote ten business letters. This sort of clearing of the decks gives me an enormous sense of relief and freedom.

Then Harold and I went for a gorgeous walk. The sweet, hot smell of spiraea surrounded us all along Morningside Road. He was able to walk fast and energetically, but at the LBI potluck last night, I listened to his persistent cough with others' ears, and grew concerned. And his hip is hurting for the first time in months. The recurrence of this old ache, after all these months, is worrisome to us both, and the anxiety spills into words that are like sandpaper on a sore.

At such times I tend to bore into Harold with questions just to break through the barrier of reserve, but as he told me later, "Sometimes I don't *know* what I feel, or why."

* After a muddy beginning the day cleared itself gradually and ended with one of those still, sunny evenings with the sky a blue bowl unstained by clouds. After supper I walked out with my Nikon along our lane and St. Charles Road. The horizontal light has such a different quality, licking along the ground subtly, lapping gently at the boulders and bushes, not blotting them with a weight of glare the way the noon sun does. Our high bush cranberry is covered with white starbursts of

flowers—tiny pinheads of blossom in the center circled with larger petals, all dappled with light, white on white, and the edges of the hairy leaves gold as the sun touches them from behind. The three days of rain have given every growing thing a startling verdancy.

✳ Coming from the office along St. Charles Road, a cement truck suddenly pulled out in front of me, blocking my lane. I braked but skidded on the rain-slick road and piled right into him—crumpling the right front end of the Peugeot, a hideous sight.

Later Harold drove the Peugeot to our body shop where it was pronounced (ironically) "undriveable." Megs sent David over with their stick shift Chevy wagon, and H. drove it home, but the effort of pushing down the stiff clutch exhausted him. In more and more pain after supper from his old kidney stone, he called Paul Parker who suggested a day in hospital on Demerol. "No Paul, let me give it a little more time." (He dreads hospitalization.) Later the pain began to fade; by morning it was gone.

A hard question faces us: Dr. Parker suggests he have the kidney stone removed. That's major surgery. Would Harold recover in time for our Cape Cod trip planned for June? Yet what if he had an attack while we're away? We'd postpone the vacation, except that so many Shaw family members are converging there just to see Harold. More and more, our plans are being dictated by illness.

✳ A morning whose clarity is pierced by birds and small boys' cries. A bumblebee large as a Ping-Pong ball careens past my face as I sit on our front step in the sun. The grass pulls away from the brick walk, close-cropped, a celadon velvet after yesterday's mowing. This is the season of grasses. Wherever I walk or drive I'm hemmed by their green hair, their lacy seed-heads all in feathery flower. Grass flower is all seed—not color but gray, dun, mint, and the lovely monochromes of green. The variety of them, cohabiting in layers, and the tender subtle shadings, make me love them. Later in the year, when heat has caked the ground, they'll persist, but the lushness and insouciance will be gone in dryness and brown. And "all flesh is grass, like a flower of the field we flourish," which means we don't flourish very long.

> *. . . but the word of our God*
> *will stand forever* (Isa. 40:6–8).

All flesh is grass
and I can feel myself growing
an inch an hour in the dark
ornamented with a lyric dew
fine as glass beads, my edges
thin as green hair.
      All flesh—
and there are seventeen kinds
of us in this one corner of the
hayfield, along with clover,
oxalis, chicory, Wild Wilber—
close enough cousins for a
succulent hay.
      Early mornings
we all smell of rain
enough to drown the microscopic
hoppers and lubricate snails
along their glistening paths:
a fine, wet fragrance, but not
so sweet as this evening, after
the noon scythe.

No longer,
now, are the windows of air
hung with our lace, embroidered
with bees. Laid low, we raise
a new incense, and under the brief
stubble, our roots grieve.

✳ Last night as we sat on the back deck after supper the sun went down, leaving us a fading radiance to talk by. (There it is again—the inevitability of dying, the drooping of flowers, the grass dried and scythed, the setting sun.) Our conversation tried to balance the elements of faith and hope with health, limited life span, and disease. There is no easy formula. Death is inevitable but not predictable. The exceptions keep proving (testing) the rule. Nor does divine healing seem to be a sure thing despite all that Harold is reading about healing being part of Christ's atonement for us.

As for us and our future, of course, hope brightens it. It is better to live in hope than despair. Is realism an even more healthy attitude, though? Madeleine says: "Don't project; things never turn out as we anticipate. We have to take, each day, what we are handed, as a present." We have been told that these are Harold's "golden months." Yes. We will take them as the gift they are.

Two

Sitting in the sun. The salmon petals of the impatiens are pearlescent (not iridescent) when seen at a certain angle—the sun refracted in each surface cell. The color is so intense it's almost vulgar, yet the silk petals are fragile—brash but vulnerable. The black iron cauldron by the front door is filled with this tender color of life.

I've been reading Psalm 30: "O Lord, I cried out to you, and you restored my health. You brought me up, O Lord, from the dead. You gave me back my life as I was going down to the grave. . . . Weeping may spend the night, but joy comes in the morning (lovely oxymoron). . . . You have turned my wailing into dancing; you have put away my sackcloth and clothed me with joy." Is it possible that such verses may turn real in Harold's life, and mine, after these months of prayer?

Reading O'Connor's letters in *The Habit of Being,* I often feel like heaving a sigh of relief. She somehow unites faith with a healthy skepticism. I can join her in saying: "Faith is what you have in the absence of knowledge. . . . This clash doesn't bother me any longer because I have got, over the years, a sense of the immense sweep . . . of creation . . . of how incomprehensible

God must necessarily be to be the God of heaven and earth. You can't fit the Almighty into your intellectual categories. . . . What kept me a skeptic in college was precisely my Christian faith: it always said wait, don't bite on this, get a wider picture, continue to read." This is precisely where I am, and my thoughts link arms with her words.

I'm challenged when she admits: "It is much harder to believe than not to believe." But I want to shout, along with her, "You must at least do this: Keep an open mind. Keep it open toward faith, keep wanting it, keep asking for it, and leave the rest to God." Which is what I have been doing—wanting, asking, waiting.

This is where H. and I follow different tracks. Somehow he finds belief simpler than I, who am a natural, life-long questioner. This is strange, because in all things except belief he tends to be more pessimistic, anticipating problems where I, in every area except belief, expect things to turn out for the best.

I don't like this role of spiritual skeptic, yet I feel it is rational, and fair—to remove the blinders, to hear the other fellow's argument, to see through others' eyes, even though this nurtures ambivalence in me. *Lord, please, lend me a sense of your reality. Then perhaps all these things will find their place in the pattern of the whole.*

✱ H. and Kris mowed most of the back lawn last evening. Then he had bad chest pains in the night. I'm fearful that some medical emergency will prevent our leaving for Cape Cod on the 13th. The trip for the purpose of a family reunion has assumed importance in all our minds; it represents normalcy and adventure both, another in our string of vacations to the east coast.

✳ A hot humid day. The shaded back deck seems a good place to write. H. continues to be nibbled at by minor symptoms which produce anxiety because of what they *may* mean—the jabs of pain from the kidney stone, the dull ache in his hip, the chest pain. If none of the above apply, he is debilitated by weakness or high blood pressure. I'm sure they're related to mental stress—decisions at HSP, working out the provisions of the will, the HSP board meeting yesterday, arrangements with a urologist for a kidney consultation, planning for the Cape, and the ongoing problem of getting cars repaired.

✳ Last night H. slept restlessly and was too tired for church. Too bad. The service would have meant a lot to him, as it did to me. Psalm 130, a psalm of Ascent, emphasizes the inevitability of human struggle—depression, bankruptcy, shame, disillusionment, loneliness, despair, ill health, financial need—all conditions which we can label "the depths" and in which we need to hear two messages: *Wait* on the Lord, *hope* in his Word.

When we're *up,* Rick suggested, we tend to talk to God from the top of our hearts—complacently. Only when we are *down,* suffocating like Jonah inside the whale, do we engage in real prayer—the kind that changes us profoundly. I keep thinking of our own realities—Harold's pain, our fears—and know this to be true. We cry to God out of extremity, not from the easy couch of comfort.

The other theme of the morning was hunger and bread. In the Lord's Prayer we ask for "daily bread"; we take into our mouths the bread and wine and "feed on them in our hearts by faith"; after Communion we thank God for feeding us with spiritual food and drink. But like physical nourishment, our spiritual food must be taken often, or we faint with hunger and grow spiritually anorexic.

I've been thinking more about hunger for God. I find it sharpest, most tantalizingly close to being satisfied, at Communion. As I am on my knees at the altar, cupped hands held up, mouth open, being fed like a baby bird, I want to stay there and feel what it is like to go on being fed. I want to prolong *the real something* that happens there.

✳ No single day seems to pass without some crisis. The dishwasher overflows, the clothes dryer won't heat, I lose my keys, Harold has hip pain.

In spite of these we're heading east at last. On the drive out of town we see trees arching over the road with sun shining through them against a dark bank of clouds. Dramatic contrast. I photograph it in my mind because the cameras and film are stowed underneath the tailgate.

✳ Woke in our cottage on the Cape to the sound of rain without wind—multiple drops landing on multiple surfaces—leaves, stones, branches, the blacktop of this little East Brewster road, sand—which produces a gentle, wet music, a kind of aural pointillism. From where I am lying in bed, I see a bird on a branch against the sky—just its dark outline—turning, contorting, preening, flicking tail and wings in the rain in a ritual of abandonment.

Later, I stroll in a mild drizzle, camera loaded with black and white film. There must be infinite possibilities for photography, but we must use what is at hand, in front of us right now. I walk down to the beach and, as I go, I make a record of seed pearl grass, wild roses filling the hedges with crumpled pink petals, the shine of rain on the sloping planes of oak leaves.

✻ Harold has been resting and reading a lot. The trip was taxing, but the quiet days are like medicine. He's had little pain, and is cheerful.

Last night after supper we walked to Ellis Landing, site of summer holidays in our early married life. I looked for one of my favorite spots which I'd photographed often—a freshet of water cutting a wide arc in the sand down to the sea. But the whole contour of the beach has changed, and with it the course of the stream, now clogged with debris.

✻ Our wedding anniversary. It seems right that we who on our Cape Cod honeymoon began to discover each other and build our marriage thirty-two years ago are still at it—in the same place! I gave Harold a postcard—a line drawing by Dana Gibson of a Victorian couple sitting on the beach, embracing ardently, with the tide rising unnoticed around their feet and legs. He loved it! And at dinner that night I read him the poem I'd written for us—"Spice."

> Sentimentalists, purists, and some
> preachers advocate marital absolutes—
> stability, a clear hierarchy for
> decision, a predictable union—
> unflawed as a blank page. No wonder
> it ends up flat. A truer wedding's
> grounded in paradox, answers the pull
> of the particular, grapples a score
> of rugged issues. Like horned toads

in Eden, incongruities add surprise
to a complacent landscape.

Thank heaven you're romantic and
irascible, I'm opinionated in my
impulsiveness. Thank God we can
lean together in our failing—a rusty
trellis propping a thorned rose.

✳ I am cherishing this time alone with Kris and Harold, alone with Harold, alone with myself. Next week it will be all family—thirty-five of us planning to come at last count. Reading Henri Nouwen's *Out of Solitude* reminds me that even Jesus found the source of strength for relationships in being alone. In Psalm 84 the psalmist says, "Those who go through the desolate valley will find it a place of springs." Balancing aloneness with gregariousness isn't easy. Both are important to me. If I were truly solitary, with no one to come to with the fruits of my solitude, it might become a barrier to being—not its precursor.

✳ Jeff drove in from New York about 12:45, all in black—pants, boots, shirt, dark glasses—an indicator of his mood, which was withdrawn. With the shortness of his visit—today and tomorrow—I want all the minutes to count, not to be trivialized. I very much want to do or say something that will make everything come right. My inability leaves a smell of failure in the air.

✳ Most of the Shaw clan is here now, wanting to be with Harold. Jeff left about an hour ago. He admitted to me before breakfast, "I'm not very happy." My prayer must not be a shallow: "Lord, make Jeff happy." This wish for him would be centered in myself, a concern not just for him but for my own peace of mind.

What I do see in him is an increasing capacity for good, for living, that is, not just for himself but beyond himself.

What he is missing, I think, is vocation. He has no call more specific than the challenge to succeed. I'm reminded of Frederick Buechner's comment: "Your vocation is to be found where your deep joy meets the world's deep need." But first you have to find the joy.

✳ While Harold was napping, I visited the deserted beach, scrubbed clean of weed and wrack by a nor'easter with winds up to fifty knots. It was like walking a snowdrift—the surface swept and molded by the irresistible air. The clouds and rain seemed to skim along about ten feet above the waves. I tried to shout and sing with the exhilaration of it, but the sound was whipped from my mouth.

So many beautiful and diverse objects—art galleries in all directions—excite me with the desire to create and possess art. Photography is a medium within my reach. I have the tools, and, I think, the eye. Being in the right place at the right time is the other ingredient, but it takes serendipity and a lot of patience.

It's like poetry. Though I know I can produce pleasing results I want more—impact, contrast, texture, abstraction, significance, not just decoration. Almost any graphic art seems more important if it is matted and mounted well. Seen alone in a field of space it achieves drama and demands attention that allows for a moment of meeting between the picture and the viewing human eye. Poetry on the page invites the same kind of attention. Pulled out from a mass of words, we can read and see it for what it is.

* Last night Harold said, happily, "The pain in my hip is better and I've no pain in my chest!" Pain gone means worry gone; we live out our days at this simplistic level. As we leave the Cape, it is with replenished mental and emotional reservoirs. But bittersweet. Will we ever be here together again?

* On our way home. With Harold driving, we emerged this morning from our Route 80 motel into a landscape of hills and valleys draped in fog. In the back seat I read through the Holy Eucharist: Rite One in the *Book of Common Prayer* and felt the grace of God at sixty miles per hour. In imagination I partook of the consecrated bread and wine and fed on it in my heart by faith. I could stay at the heart's altar rail as long as I wished, and worshiped in the Presence. Reading the Prayers of the People I prayed for Jeff and wrote this:

> God, cajole and nudge him, draw,
> delight, and dream him close,
> drift him along love's eddy, dare him,
> inch him to yourself and with each inch,
> yield him a yard of joy. Touch him;
> with tears teach him.
> Tangle his thoughts in yours

And realized the words were for me, too.

Three

─────────────────────────────────

Through my tears, you are teaching me, Lord. Like Jeff, I need your patient instruction in living in this place where I have never walked before.

Being home again is like opening a hotel window over a city street—the noise floods in and immerses us. Bills to be paid, laundry to be done, phone calls to be returned, films to be developed, groceries to be bought, an overrun garden to be set to rights (catnip took over the rock garden, the violas dried themselves to death, the new beans were neatly trimmed to the ground by rabbits).

✳ These days are a patchwork. Harold is in constant discomfort—either hip or chest pain. John, home after completing his internship, thinks the chest pain is an esophageal reflux of stomach acid, and he has put wooden blocks under the head of our bed to reduce the problem, which means we slide down to the foot by morning.

To compound the matter, H. can't seem to tell me what he

wants to eat, so the responsibility is mine. Should he stick to plain food that suits him best—boiled potatoes, fish, or fruits, or salads? But when I prepare them, he barely picks at them.

These small physical harrassments are like ulcers which won't heal. They erode his peace of mind. They wear away at me, too, though he has no idea how much. And another decision affected by Harold's condition: Will he be strong enough to attend the Booksellers Convention in Dallas this year?

On the plus side there was Lauren's prayer: "Lord Jesus, give me an angel," and a wonderful morning with John at Town House Books—he, buying a year's worth of reading for his new assignment at the Naval base hospital in Iwakuni, Japan. Later, I put the finally final touches to *Postcard,* then John walked me through the process of printmaking in the darkroom. I got so excited that, even after he'd gone to bed, I stayed up making print after print of my Cape Cod photos.

✱ H. lay in bed looking forlorn this morning and said, "Would you pray for me?" I asked for time to read my Bible first, hoping to find a meaningful verse to build a prayer around. Failing in this, I prayed for him out of a sense of powerlessness and personal bankruptcy. A cry for help, awkward and embarrassing in its poverty. No faith in it, only obedience.

We prayed, too for our HSP team, on their way to CBA in our wagon. It's still uncertain whether Harold will fly down with me on Sunday. His hip and leg pain are disabling. A further complication is hoarseness; besides the frustration of not being able to clear his throat, it makes him *sound* weak and infirm.

✻ In honor of John's twenty-seventh birthday, which he'll spend in Japan in August, we ate lunch out. Afterwards he put on his uniform and posed for pictures on the deck. Then we all prayed together in the bedroom. It was a kind of good-bye—a necessary step in John's life journey.

But my leaving for CBA without Harold seems a desertion. In another sense, however, the distance will buffer my anxiety about each small symptom. I am fine-tuned to his pain, and getting away to a busy convention will exchange this tension for another kind—renting a car, finding my way around a strange and complex city, long days of meeting people in the convention center—some of the firsts of acting and being on my own. But I must learn. *Teach me, Lord.*

✻ My fears about the minutiae of the trip were unfounded. Everything went like clockwork. The baggage came through. I rented a little white Chevette and, with the aid of a map, followed the route through Dallas to my exit and motel. When I called Harold, I could hear his disappointment in missing his first CBA in twenty years. Soon after, the rest of the HSP gang—Megs, Randy, Sandy, and Terri—crowded into my room, eating ice cream cones, zany with fatigue. They read me the poem they had group-composed in the car on the way down, containing such deathless lines as: "This landscape is supremely dull/a rock or two, and then a lull."

Now I'm learning the joys and struggles of the independent woman. After a day on the convention floor, I "sallied forth" to the Anatole and *Guidepost*'s fortieth anniversary party—driving in the maze of fast-moving freeways, joining a cocktail party, seeing old friends.

Roy Carlisle of *Harper's* came by and we talked about "the Episcopal experience." I saw Richard Foster, who gave me a warm, comforting hug, and we had fifteen minutes of the kind of conversation that happens a lot at CBA—skipping the pleasantries and plunging immediately to the heart of matters. He wants a meeting of like minds—Calvin Miller, Karen, myself, others, to meet, pray, and minister to each other.

I called Harold from the convention floor. After another night of chest pain he admitted, "I'm facing some realities. I think the cancer may have invaded my neck and chest." It is rare for him to let such discouragement into his voice. My heart plummeted. The whole day was agony—greeting people with a cheerful smile, talking books, making business contacts— with that ache of fear underneath. That evening, at the airport, I called him again. He was encouraged by the doctor's diagnosis of his hoarseness—a simple inflammation of his vocal chords, which seems to be unrelated to the cancer.

I found a small chapel and went into the stillness. I thanked the Lord for helping me through the week. It is comforting to know that I can handle the travel, the decision-making, the navigating alone. Sales are brisk and enthusiasm for new projects high—all reasons for thanksgiving. Then, before boarding the plane for home, I prayed for Harold—a mix of relief and longing.

✱ "The purpose of any of God's promises is its fulfillment— he is eager to fulfill it." Harold has just read this quote by F. F. Bosworth, from *Christ the Healer*. I know he is just as eager to claim the promise of healing as God is to voice it. So what is the block? What keeps God's eagerness and Harold's acceptance from joining in wholeness?

I'm not very patient with him. An outburst from me two weeks ago about his need to be responsible for taking his own medications evidently shocked him into an awareness of them for a day or two, but after I left for Dallas he ignored the daily packages of vitamins and the bark tea I had prepared ahead of time. It's hard to find the balance. I want to care for him but I don't think it's good for him to abdicate all responsibility for his own health. I am a confusion of love and frustration. I almost feel that if he wanted it badly enough, he could grow into health again. That's irrational, I know.

* Weeding the beans. Great handfuls of tall green invaders come up easily, root and all, as I bend and stoop and stretch, the small gnats buzzing intimately in my ears. The sprinkler is giving the new grass a good soaking. The young beans are a couple of inches long—supple, slim, hanging in vertical warps, decorated with purple. This garden work heals me. Ordering my world, feeling its vitality, helping and cooperating with it brings me a hope that I can feel but not explain.

Once again Harold's symptoms are changing. His leg, he says, is "perfect"—quite pain-free. His voice is hoarse but his chest pain has left. Now there is a sharp, localized stab in his left shoulder blade that reaches round and under his arm. Dr. Parker suggests moist heat, but what good is moist heat against cancer? A doctor has to suggest something. He can't tell a patient, "Look, there are no answers, no medications for you. You'll just have to live through it. Or die through it."

In bed Harold lets the pain move from his shoulder into his soul. I can feel him taking it in, weighing its meaning: "I guess if the cancer is in my bones, it will just slowly incapacitate me." He is reversing his earlier denial. And where is faith in the equation? Can we still believe that the sequence of pains in leg, chest, kidney, back, are fiery darts of the Enemy and that "raising the shield of faith" will protect his body?

I complained to him this morning, that he hadn't smoothed his hair down after shampooing. His new growth of hair is iron gray, thick and bushy. It stands up straight on top, and when he lies down the back of his head becomes a giant cowlick. I

117

said, only partly in jest, "I want you to look handsome and well-groomed and strong." He just leaned his head against me mournfully, "Oh, honey. Oh, honey."

* I saw a face in a thunderhead this afternoon—a strong masculine face with jutting chin and nose—watched it all the way as I drove home from the office. The nose turned bulbous and split from the face, the chin receded, the human likeness disappeared. It was like seeing someone eroded by illness. *Harold, stay recognizable, whole, a little longer.*

Four

I find the Eucharist a time of breaking barriers—between me and God, me and my brothers and sisters, me and myself. The broken bread required the breaking of Christ's spirit, and taking it in, with understanding, breaks *our* hearts. Our fiercely arrogant, independent selves crumble with the crumbling of the loaf. And in some mysterious way, this brokenness brings a new kind of wholeness.

Along the highways, growing out of the broken sod, the summer flowers have replaced spring's feather grass-heads which so fascinated me. Farther in from the road, where the soil is richer, the Queen Anne's lace whitens the banks with its small circles of lace. The effect of the multiple flower heads floating against green, with touches of pink clover, the yellow of daisies, is like a living painting—a Seurat shimmering in noon heat. Ironic, that such beauty can bloom in the kind of gravelly ground in which I find myself struggling.

God, am I slipping away from you again? There has been no direct word from you in the Bible lately. The expectations of others galvanize me into action—everyone's expectations, that is, except yours. You are a Gentleman—patient, allowing my lack of you to make me conscious of my dryness.

119

✷ A letter from John with the details a mother longs for—housing, food, weather, etc. In the same mail we got his zany message sent by Navy radio to a local receiver, then typed and forwarded to us. It read "Arrived Iwakuni. Have turned Buddhist, married Japanese girl, sold all personal effects. More later."

✷ Harold's pattern of sequential pain has shown up again. A new low-back pain has replaced the ulcer-like chest pains during the last twenty-four hours. I sense withdrawal on his part, a reluctance to comment, to talk at all. His typical posture these days is bolt upright in a chair, head bowed, expression puzzled, yet resigned—downcast, inward, hard to penetrate. I tell him again and again how much I love him, how close I want to be to him, whether he can talk or not.

✷ At noon today we visited Dr. Reid, a local oncologist. Much as we both love Liz Hillman, we feel we need someone close, so that our time and energy are not depleted by the long drive downtown. The doctor seemed sensible, a good listener, but without Liz's feisty humor. He scheduled bloodwork and scans for Thursday.

Tonight I feel thoroughly tenderized. The enzyme is pain, which reached down into me yesterday, through old, unhealed wounds. I cried all day—for the cancer, the unknowing, the dark future. I cried about my struggles to keep up with the work, my need to learn new, difficult tasks. I cried for John's leaving, for Jeff's coming home, for Harold's pain, for Kris's moods, for my dryness, for my search for God and reality. And when I stopped crying I tried to find balance and rationality and couldn't and wanted to die. It was purgation and left me clean—washed, flat, and dry as sand at low tide, but rinsed clean by my own tears.

✱ Called Dr. Reid's office today for the third time to learn Harold's test results. We're still in the dark. Is the doctor saying, in effect, "Well, the patient is stable, so no hurry to begin treatment" or "There are significant changes, but Shaw seems optimistic so we may as well allow him the bliss of his ignorance a little longer."

Dr. Reid finally returned our call: "Mr. Shaw, after studying your test results and comparing them with earlier tests from January and April, I can find no significant change—no new tumor growth. In fact, your CEA level has declined from 270 to 250—not a large change, but in the right direction. Call on me if you have any new symptoms."

We can scarcely believe it. What a great birthday gift! Saturday is Harold's sixty-ninth and the celebrations string out through the weekend—HSP's party with cakes decorated to look like the *Bible Handbook* and the *Promise Book*; dinner at the Kuhnes' Friday; croquet on the Mains' lawn Saturday, until it is too dark to see the wickets; cake with Harold on Sunday with just our family. Then, prayer at the Bosches in the afternoon. A picture stays with me—Georgia reaching out and taking Kris's hand to draw her into the circle of intercession and thankfulness.

✱ In the morning sun, the roadsides call to be photographed. The chicory blue is vivid, surrounded by Queen Anne's lace in multiple-sized flowerheads. The older flowers are beginning to enclose, as the ribs that anchor each floweret in the head bend inward at the top and hold in a cup the mass of tiny petals and flowers turning to seed—a birdcage shape that persists all winter, catching flower cupfuls of snow. Some of the grass seedheads are fat and woolly, like caterpillars, with the bright light behind them outlining their thick fuzz.

After taking Kris to the office where she is working part-time, I stopped near a little lake whose banks were thickly covered with wild prairie growth in full bloom. The chicory is that innocent, airy, early morning blue that solidifies and darkens as it withers by noon. The clover is a pure, deep mauve. The buttercups and Indian paintbrush glow with an intense yellow that not only reflects light but beams from within—a self-illuminating pigmentation. And the Queen Anne's lace is a lavishing of medallions and copyrighted patterns decorating the dry, often littered wasteland of weeds. Photographing them against the glitter of the lake fortified me against the exigencies of the day, and my moods—too easily elated or depressed—"labile" as John puts it.

✳ Sunday, in church, one line from a hymn—"Let old unfaith not hold my soul"—hit me hard because I need to guard against my old patterns of skepticism and despair.

My attention was caught this morning by a quote from St. Augustine, that the self is "a narrow house, too narrow for Thee to enter. Oh, make it wide. If it is in ruins, rebuild it." I feel that narrowness, trapped in my own sensibilities. My patterns of thought and life are so tied into my central self—spokes of a wheel with self at the hub. Though it has formed as a self-protective structure to wall out destruction, too often I shut out God too.

✳ A letter from John with this newly-written poem:

Unless
I die disheartened
I see no greater joy
than laying down this hungry shell,
than laying down this black hole hell
of body to the soil

Until,
while standing cleanly,
I glance back through my soul
at appetites so long unmet,
at pride, at lust, and gray regret
left lying in the hole.

Unless
I am mistaken
all of us wait for this:
to jettison the grasping hands,
to lope through new-created lands
where hope and have may kiss.

"If we have hope for what we do not yet have, we wait for it
patiently" (Rom. 8:25).

"Mom," he wrote, "it's a rather dark poem, but it expresses
the groan in Romans 8. I'm praying for you each day—for
courage, endurance, hope, encouragement. Hang in there.
John"

I answered his letter immediately. "I stood in my office this
morning, opened your letter and cried as I read the poem. The
last line dissolved me. It is the cry of all of us for all that we
don't have, and hope for. I'll pray for temporary easing of, or
satisfaction of, those unfading appetites, but our deeper hunger
will only be satisfied when we are 'liberated from bondage to
decay.' I'm fascinated that the frustration of our situation is not

our choice but God's. It's as if he says, 'Suffer the frustration. Struggle and starve and weep. By contrast, the freedom I plan for your eternal future will seem even more glorious.'"

But my brave words to John are only a whispered hope.

Five

A bizarre anniversary—a year today since Harold's first hospitalization. I feel like a zero, or a question mark.

The Bosches come in the afternoon. I confess my feelings, but they think of me only as a deeply godly woman. No matter what I say, they can't fathom my ambivalence, which I must begin to deal with.

When I asked Karen, later, to recommend a good psychotherapist, she told me of someone who is taking a couple of new clients. Even the thought of unloading brings relief.

* My time this morning with the therapist, Terry Allen, was intense—an avalanche of feelings, moods, beliefs, doubts, fears. She echoed my own conclusion that I can't experience the reality of God because I don't feel my own reality. I am a shell of performance—Christian behavior masking a shifting center. Her avowed aim is to help me see in myself what Christ *has formed in me*. She says she discerns integrity in me. And I *am* honest. But I don't feel integrated. She wonders if my mood

swings are hormonal. My poetry she views as an activity that achieves tangible results—a proof to myself that I am worthwhile.

One of the fears that surface is of betrayal. Terry suggested I fear abandonment if Harold dies, abandonment by God, too. And, while preparing myself for Harold's possible death is a major adjustment, having him in remission also takes considerable readjustment. I like Terry. She listens, and remembers. I trust her.

✳ Harold moaned and tossed in the night—overwhelmed with angst about HSP's future, the burden seeming greater because of his diminished energy to deal with it. In the morning he read to me from Psalm 20—a prayer to establish one's purpose, one's heart desire. We both applied it to our company, Harold's life, my own unanchored heart.

> May the Lord answer you when you are in
>   distress;
> may the name of the God of Jacob protect you.
> May he send you help from the sanctuary
> and grant you support from Zion.
> May he give you the desire of your heart
> and make all your plans succeed.
> May the Lord grant all your requests.
> Some trust in chariots and some in horses,
> but we trust in the name of the Lord our God.

At dinner with Vic and Dixie Oliver, we talked a lot about spiritual depression. Vic made a good analogy: Just as the relationship in a marriage ebbs and flows, yet holds firm because of prior commitment, even when there is disagreement and love seems to have left, so too, because of prior commitment, we are held in continual relationship with God whether or not our level of faith is high, whether or not we *feel* that he is with us.

* The skids of *Postcard from the Shore* were delivered by truck today. I opened one up. The front cover picture of shells glinting through salt water looked wet enough to smell under the laminate. I'm happy the print work is good, and I've found no typos yet. But there's a curious sense of anticlimax—the project is over; the creative frenzy exorcised; the product is irreversible. I am left with this object. Will people be able to see the shore through my eyes?

* The days are shortening. We used to have all evening's light to walk by. Now we have to hurry dinner to walk before dark. Tonight the half-moon is high, the sky's blue is filmy with fibers and tendrils of cloud wrapping the stars. Planes wink like fireflies from north, south, east, west. The view is never duplicated.

On one of our evening strolls down St. Charles Road we saw Lindy, our young neighbor, taking out the garbage. We stopped and talked to her. Today a letter came:

> I'm not quite sure what's leading me to write but tonight when I talked with you both, something inside me reached out to you. I saw you walking, arm in arm, and it brought tears to my eyes. I felt such compassion at the sight of you.
>
> For twenty-two years I've despised anything to do with Christianity and God. Last year the hypocrisy of it all came out and more than ever I doubted. I wanted to end my life last summer because of what

happened between my parents, but I refused to give up. A couple of months ago I decided that I would quit trying to find happiness aside from God, and told myself I'd give up everything if I could be sure that he is real. In the midst of hypocrisy and worldliness I have decided to look to God and not to those who have made him a joke. Tonight I saw and felt God in your presence. When you told us, Mr. Shaw, that you were praying for us, I almost fainted. You, coming close to dying. You, praying for us.

I just want to let you know that seeing you both walking down the hill and loving each other fills my soul like nothing else. You are proof that God does not walk away from marriage, and you didn't walk away from God . . . Though I am only a beginner at this, I do know God wanted me to take out the garbage tonight for a good reason.

Love, Lindy.

✱ We are emplaned, arc-ing our way through the air across the continent towards Bellingham and Robin, our first-born. Harold has scarcely smiled or spoken. Does he feel any joy or enthusiasm at the prospect of a week away? Is the problem this—that he knows he cannot leave his pain behind? And that he may never make this trip again? Often I am unable to read this partner of my heart.

Wet weather clamped down on us as soon as we arrived. Next morning, though, H., Lindsay and I walked along Squallicum Lake Road and the sun gleamed briefly in and out. Through my camera film flowed freely, etched with grasses, fine and pale and lacy, and bold spears of brown bracken. The brave color of raspberry leaves. The apple trees buttoned all over with rosy fruit. A reddish barn hugging the ground in front of a foothill. A few brilliant maples, with indigo hills behind.

✳ Suffered a touch of cabin fever yesterday morning. Mark and Robin's farmhouse—charming, cheerful, cozy—is cramped for five people. Fed H. some oatmeal, then spent a blissful hour alone, walking the rising and falling ribbon of Jensen Road, and snapping the shutter. At first the sun was low, hidden, and I tried to get the subtle brilliance of the leaves without sun—luminous from within themselves. It had rained during the night and the air was cool and sharp with the damp, fungal smell of wet woods, the dun colors sparked with the burning coals of leaves. I think I took some of the best shots of my life. Then the sun came out—dramatically bright against the heavy hills under the low frown of clouds. It's the contrast that is so heady, and being alone and filled with a singing sense of "It's here, now, this freshness, the glory of sky and conifer and rotting deadfall, this rich humus of life." I went back along Squallicum Lake Road, high on country air.

✳ This morning we made an early start by car for Anacortes and the San Juan Islands ferry. Now I'm sitting in the car alone, writing, editing a Madeleine manuscript, enjoying the healing solitude. All the other passengers are up on the observation decks, including Harold in his cocoon of silence. Thanks or response from him are rare. I ache for myself and for him. How can he remain aloof and distant surrounded by loving family and all this beauty? Yet if I mention it, I might seem negative too. All I can do is love him and care for him as hard as I can, and hang on to my own sense of well-being—

strong right now, but like this Northwest weather, subject to change.

✱ Before returning to West Chicago, we met Carl and Betsy Armerding at a restaurant midway between Bellingham and Vancouver for a Canadian Thanksgiving dinner. Betsy told me of a vision a friend had seen of her in prayer—a flowing, clear river with sediment at the bottom but with the sun, sky, and trees reflected on its surface. Which should we focus on, the sludge or the surface? Both must be kept in balance—the dark things in a life honestly confronted without ignoring the beauty.

✱ Terry feels that my heart-longings are the mind of Christ in me calling out for my health and wholeness. I am learning to talk to her, to flow with language and illusion and feeling, to admit when a topic is a dead end, or when we're touching on something important. With her, I can cry when I feel full of tears and not be embarrassed, knowing it's a clue to what is significant to me.

Later, back at the office, I was reading biblical metaphors in preparation for my St. Mark's retreat message and among them I came across "The Lord thy God in the midst of thee is mighty." The mind of Christ Terry sees in me. The reflection of sky Betsy's friend saw in her. What other realities are we blind to in ourselves?

The words of a long-ago quilter ring true: "I make them warm to keep my family from freezing. I make them beautiful to keep my heart from breaking."

Her poignant paradox nudges me into a new poem which I'm calling "Quiltmaker."

To keep a husband and five children warm,
she quilts them covers thick as drifts against
the door. Through every fleshy square the white
    threads
needle their almost invisible tracks; her hours
count each small suture that holds together
the raw-cut, uncolored edges of her life.

She pieces each one beautiful, and summer-
    bright,
to thaw her frozen soul. Under her fingers
the scraps grow to green birds, and purple,
improbable leaves; deeper than calico, her mid-
    winter mind
bursts into flowers. She watches them unfold
between the double stars, the wedding rings.

✱ I was up early, and at St. Mark's by 9:00 A.M. About forty
women came to the retreat—a varied and remarkable group,
as it turned out.

My talk on "Living Metaphorically" took an hour, after
which we divided into five groups to discuss the questions I'd
prepared.

At lunch each participant introduced her left-hand neighbor
with a metaphor. One woman was described as "a rubber raft,
flexible, and easy to climb onto in trouble." Another was "a
piece of mahogany that is rich and beautiful, and will be even
more so as God carves it into his chosen shape."

✱ Harold said this morning, "I think the cancer's showing up
in my collarbone." Nothing is visible, but the spot is

excruciatingly tender to the touch. We went to St. Mark's early for the healing Eucharist, a great effort because the stress of getting up and off in a hurry gives H. muscle spasms. Karen was there, and several gathered around and laid hands on him as Carl Brenner anointed him with oil and prayed.

Coming out of church I greeted a close friend who looked at me and then turned away without a word as if she couldn't be bothered to speak. I felt a pang of hurt, and knew immediately that this slight—real or imagined—could trigger an onslaught of depression. When H. and I stopped on the way home to buy milk at the Blue Goose in St. Charles, he handed me a twenty dollar bill with a smile and the remark, "D'you know why I always like to give you more than you'll need? Because I love you!" His words, sweeter because of the earlier sting, melted me to tears and I cried all the way to the Bosches, during our prayer time, and later at home. Fearful of going all the way down into depression—to disbelief and thoughts of self-destruction—I called Terry, who agreed to see me first thing tomorrow.

✳ Terry's concern was like balm in Gilead. "You need comfort as well as counsel," she said. "You're going through a really tough time." It felt good to cry with her, to be able to describe my feelings as I was having them instead of talking about them after the fact. Terry believes that depression is a healthy sign. Like pain, it tells us that something is wrong. It's not neurotic, but is usually a response to some kind of loss. Because everything feels like a huge problem, counseling is valuable for sorting through and discovering what is significant and what is minor. Depression, she thinks, can be a catalyst for finding solutions. In addition, she feels that I need to become my own best friend and engage in inner discourse, to balance things out, and to accept the paradoxes in myself—like John Donne's "strong Christian faith and raging doubt."

✳ Steve Board has accepted the job as VP/General Manager of Shaw! He'll assume responsibility at the office after December 5. As a result Harold felt better this afternoon—no pain for the first time in weeks, and more energy, "as if someone had turned a key."

IV

HOARFROST AND ASHES
November 1985–January 1986

> Knight: *I want knowledge, not faith, not supposition, but knowledge. I want God to stretch out his hand towards me, to reveal himself and speak to me.*
>
> Death: *But he remains silent.*
>
> Knight: *I call out to him in the dark, but no one seems to be there.*
>
> Death: *Perhaps no one is there.*
>
> Knight: *Then life is an outrageous horror. No one can live in the face of death knowing that all is nothing.*
>
> —INGMAR BERGMAN, **The Seventh Seal**

One

"To be in a place of pain forces us not only to face risky and uncomfortable realities but to cry out for help beyond ourselves," writes Lanney Mayer in a letter. "Our realities are the creeping chaos of human aging, disease, decay, erosion of our security, our implicit separateness, our personal failure, our superficiality, the stench of surrounding evil. What we want in our pain are *solutions,* but often all we get is a *response*: God is, and God cares, as we face and touch life's boundaries."

Lanney quotes Lewis in *The Problem of Pain*: "God whispers to us in our pleasures, speaks to us in our conscience, and shouts to us in our pain." *Lord, am I deaf that I can't hear you shouting? I want to hear the roar of the massed crowd of witnesses in Hebrews 12.* The Bible imagery is neither dumb nor inert; why doesn't it overwhelm me? Why is my imagination not more stirred and energized? All I do in these days is plod, keep the continuum going; ask and ask Harold the same questions: "Is the pain still bad?" "How did you sleep?" "Are you feeling any stronger?" "Did you take your vitamins?" "What would you like to eat?" "What can I do to make you feel better?"

* After a miserable night, Harold asked me to make an appointment with Paul Parker. We're trying to link cause and effect, to track the pain with regard to eating, sitting, lying down, coughing, shortness of breath. Nothing seems consistent. H. fears he's losing ground. And after injecting novocaine and cortisone into the sore spot in his chest, Dr. Parker suggests we try oxygen at night.

So tonight we are sleeping with a new friend—an oxygen tank big as a rocket standing in the corner of the bedroom. It supplies Harold with oxygen through a nasal cannula, a flexible plastic tube. All night we hear its soft, splashy sound as it bubbles through a bottle of distilled water. It certainly seems to relieve him of the strangled, suffocating feeling that lying down has caused.

* This morning at the Adult Sunday school class Bob Webber's teaching on worship was illuminating. He warned us of the perils of approaching the liturgy and the Eucharist intellectually or analytically. One thought stuck with me: as our spirits reach out to God, and his Spirit reaches toward us, each responds to the other and we meet in symbols—particularly the bread and wine. I carried that thought with me to Communion.

Rick's sermon was on Elijah—a man being refined by suffering. The name of the town, *Zarephath*—where he helped a widow, is, by definition, the place of refinement. The means for God's provision for him were all so faulty—an unclean raven, an old, poor widow, a handful of cracked corn. But God used them. As he uses cancer, and arguments, and rain.

I also liked what he said about the three-and-a-half year drought in Israel. It was not so much a punishment as a demonstration of what it *felt like* to be deprived of the rain of God's blessing—a sign, a parable of the meaning of God's absence. In the afternoon Rick came over with Communion, a sign of God's presence for Harold.

* Today I asked Harold a question which has lived in the back of my mind ever since we left our Plymouth Brethren assembly two years ago and began looking for a new church: Why did you do it? Why did you leave your place of leadership and influence, the church group we both grew up in? Why did you give up the battle to change the legalism and narrowness from within the group, trying to be genuine salt and light? I knew some of the obvious problems, which we had both discussed with the elders after H.'s resignation—the lack of freedom for the work of the Spirit, the energy wasted on infighting, the resistance to teaching on "charismatic" gifts and ministry and worship. But I felt there was another, unexpressed reason for his decisions.

He looked me in the eye with love and a glint of satisfaction. "I knew what I wanted for you—that your gifts and insights might find more appreciation and outlet, that you would have opportunity to enrich others publicly. All my life I've been able to participate fully, to be a leader among God's people. And I want all of that for you. It can happen at St. Mark's."

I am profoundly moved. What a gift! I resolved that such a present wouldn't be neglected but acted upon.

* Dr. Parker called with the results of last week's blood tests. H.'s red blood count is good, proportion of new cells is good, but his CEA has jumped to 520 from the last reading of 250 in late August. H. didn't seem too surprised. He feels in himself the increasing weakness and pain of cancer and this only

confirmed in a different way what his body had already told him.

* I'm sitting in the family room, alone and quiet, listening to a tape of the Wheaton Men's Glee Club, turned low. The soft sound of rain surrounds the house, and it pours a slow, bittersweet quality on this hour. It's good for us both to be alone now, to go through a time of silence, a withdrawal in gray regret, an opportunity to let the sadness settle into our spirits without a false attempt at distraction or levity. This is real. It's not a dream. I have a disease- and pain-ridden husband whose distress sometimes blocks our free intercourse.

The flow between us lately has been jerky and constrained. But the news about the CEA reading has brought us eyeball to eyeball with the inroads of cancer again. We are both dealing with it internally, separately. Now we must face and work through it together.

* Saturday afternoon I baked a fragrant cheese-onion bread, and at 6:00 we picked up Karen and David and took them, the bread, and assorted cheeses to the Lobs, who had prepared a Sabbath meal for us. All ten of our Group were there—our circle of heart-friends. It was very moving to sit with them around the candlelit table, to salt and pass the bread, and drink the wine together—not Communion, though the eucharistic overtones were inevitably present, but a Jewish meal of soup, dried fruits and nuts, breads and cheeses. Rick told us of his new conviction about the efficacy of holy oil and water in prayer and healing, and we talked about how symbol and reality overlap and reinforce each other. Harold spoke out in hoarse, measured syllables, halting between words and phrases for breath, but with an almost prophetic authority, putting into words how deeply symbol has affected his thinking and his sense of the reality of intangible things; that symbols give us *access* to the ineffable. I was profoundly touched to hear him voice these ideas with such difficulty, yet power.

On the way home H. was calm—said he'd been pain-free all evening. Sunday he was well enough to come to the second service, though as I watched him sitting next to me, his profile drawn in sharp relief by the light from the stained-glass window, I thought his cheek looked more sunken, his face thin and gray.

We sang some hymns and songs from the new hymnal, including an antiphon during Communion, "Wait for the Lord, his day is near; wait for the Lord, be strong, take heart," which entered me and softened and salved my soul pain.

✱ John called from Iwakuni, fatigued and discouraged with the way some things were going in Japan. This was a blow to Harold. He lay in bed crying "Oh Lord, help me," over and over, "I'm too weak to battle for John." H. who has so often been strong and able for me now needs me to be strong and able for him. Somehow, this antiphonal comfort is made available. We take turns undergirding each other. It's a dance to a minor tune.

✱ Yesterday H. was so weak he almost passed out in the shower, and I had to dry him off as he leaned against the tiled wall. At night I can feel a faint tremor in him, a hum, a vibration, like an appliance that's not squarely balanced.

I called Dr. Reid's office with our decision to resume the

chemo as soon as they could schedule it. It's to be done this week, so maybe H. will get over it by Thanksgiving.

✳ Harold—admitted, gowned, weighed, and settled in bed— is in our local hospital for this new cis-platinum chemo treatment.

On the road back home to fetch his robe and slippers, I stopped the car on impulse, left it parked on the gravel shoulder, and dove impulsively with camera into the prickly, thickly-bristling elderberry undergrowth just southeast of Van Kampen's brook.

An unseasonably warm rain the night before had been stopped in its tracks by a sudden cold wave so that everything flowing, running free, was swiftly solidified as by the wand of the White Witch of Narnia.

Through all the sloping woods bordering the road the small creeks and streams formed by the torrent of rain had been drowning the layered, copper-brown leaves. With the cold— temperatures plummeting from a mild sixty-five degrees to ten below—the swirls and eddies of water froze so fast that their lovely, abstract lines and curves are now perfectly preserved. My camera caught the leaves embedded in crystal or lifted on crests of paralyzed rainwater. When the air seeps under ice, its shape shows white, so that every bubble and ripple is outlined and highlighted. The thin skin of baroque ice, from which the water has now drained away, created a sculpture striking as Orrefors lead crystal.

The air is so still and sunny, with the ping of frost still in it, but I know how impermanent ice can be, like joy, like health, like life. Even if it warms up tomorrow, though, the images of ice will stay frozen on my film and I can repeat this moment of wonder, this epiphany, whenever I wish, as I look at my slides.

When I returned to the hospital, H. was sedated and dozing.

✻ Now that Steve is officially with us, I have written a press release and compiled an announcement list. Went on to see Terry. She feels that as I have internalized some of Harold's characteristics—stability, logic, etc.—I have confirmed their value but grown beyond my need of them *in him*. She suggested I read and meditate on Galatians 6:2: "Carry each other's burdens and in this way you will fulfill the law of Christ." With regard to the balance between carrying others' burdens as a means of feeling worthy and finding value in oneself: "Let each one examine his own work [or himself] and then he can celebrate [boast, take pride in] himself without comparing himself to someone else, for each one should carry his own load." This seemed revolutionary to me—finding in myself cause for celebration!

✻ With Harold back home after the awful chemo ordeal, I keep trying to get fluids into him. We deal in very small victories—three tablepoonfuls of chicken soup swallowed and kept down, a dab of ice cream.

He groans a lot, saying under his breath, "God help me." But God doesn't seem to help him.

Our night was one long interruption. He coughs weakly but frantically, trying to clear his lung of mucus, which is blood-flecked. He must either start or stop the oxygen, or go to the bathroom, or have his pillows rearranged, or take (and gag on) pain pills, or move from bed to chair, and back.

He rarely says thank you, or seems aware of my fatigue. Once after I lashed back at him, I sat down with him and said, "I failed the acid test, didn't I?" He just looked at me, saying nothing. I'm used to looking to him for help at times like these when I need to deliver my soul from guilt. But he can grant me no absolution; his malaise has cut him off from me, and I must prepare to be cut off even more drastically.

✱ Yesterday was our all-day editorial retreat—here, so I could be part of it. There were seven of us, including Steve. I was on the run all day, upstairs to try to slip food into H. who is so weak that sometimes I'm petrified that he's *gone*.

Dr. Reid called to report that there are indistinct changes in the lower left chest. He suspects it is a new tumor.

H. has been having mini-nightmares whenever he drops off to sleep—fears about what the drugs are doing to him. He often seems on the borderline of irrationality, and can't concentrate enough to read and pray. I feel essentially alone. It's the hardest part of the whole bleak process. Kris is casually affectionate, but uninvolved (a defense against her own pain?), and there is no Harold to take Harold's place. I pour out my pain to Terry. After all, I am paying her to hear me, but once a week doesn't take care of it. God is still silent.

Rick came with Communion and holy oil today. He says I must look for Christ in people. I made a confession to him about my Sunday outburst to H.—so unfair, so explosive, so irresistible. He understood my resentment of this drawn-out hopelessness and loneliness, laid hands on me, and absolved me of guilt.

I napped and cried, and napped and cried. Then checked H.; he was reading a book!

✱ Since Rick's visit, Harold has improved, beginning his climb out of the pit of weakness. His will has been engaged again. Tuesday I went to work in the afternoon and came home to find he'd showered, shaved, and washed his hair.

The forces have gathered for Turkey day. The Kussros, Jeff, Kris, Dave, Graham, and finally Tom and Kathy Burrows. When the feast was ready, Karl and I went up to get Harold. Karl came down the stairs first, with H.'s hand bearing down on his shoulder, his other arm hooked around my waist. It was his first entry into the world of the first floor for a week. I asked if he were well enough to say grace. He shook his head and asked Jeff, who prayed at length and with feeling—a blessing indeed. I carved the turkey myself, for the first time. And Harold ate a small but complete meal. Thanksgiving!

One of the day's best blessings was the sealed letter Karen handed me Wednesday afternoon. In part it read: "I thank God that you have trusted me with some of your griefs. I have felt privileged to be counted a burden-bearer. Even your reproof about constancy, which I know was hard for you [to say], were words good for me to hear. I thank God that you take time to photograph ice patterns and that you make poetry in relationships as well as in words, and for your exuberance, and the way you love things deeply, and see the world passionately, and seek God extravagantly."

✳ H. dozes his way through the hours. Still, he, Marian, Jeff, and I spent Saturday afternoon going over finances, insurance, taxes, both business and personal, while I made extensive notes. I'm pleased with Jeff's patience and help—listening to H.'s whispered, slow words on into the evening, taking out the garbage, doing dishes.

✳ Saw Terry today for an hour and a half—a measured, reflective time. She helps me to see the difference between being "fallen," and being finite, or human. My finiteness often makes me doubt my value. Yet Adam and Eve, before the Fall, were as limited as I, and it was their reaching beyond those limits, their coveting infinitude, which constituted their sin. In imagination we can always project beyond our own finiteness into something larger. That is why the imagination needs to be sanctified; it has the potential for both holiness and hellishness.

Terry is concerned that I know what to do if Harold dies—things like calling the doctor or the paramedics. She advised me, also, to talk *now* to Rick about funeral arrangements, since H. said yesterday he wanted Rick in charge. This kind of preparation could seem morbid. I feel, though, that I must step onto a bridge of reality which will help me across the dividing stream between wife and widow.

✳ Today I urged and pushed Harold until he got up, showered, and shaved. He walked from room to room. If he doesn't, his muscles will continue to waste away. Yet I know it's just a delaying tactic. As it is, he sits most of the time, with eyes half-closed and with little interest in what goes on around him. This lethargy seems an enemy, but perhaps it's more like anesthesia; though it cuts off communication, it deadens pain.

Yet tonight he sat in his chair and cried. "I hate for you to have to do so much for me. I'm so helpless. I hate that too." Later he repeated to me over and over in his hoarse whisper, "I love you so much." I store up the words in my heart, the fire-flashes of love in his eyes.

He expresses his puzzlement at the implacability of the disease, and his progressive weakness. "If the Lord really is the Healer, and has given all these promises, and I've claimed them in praying faith, why don't I recover?" It's hard for me to watch his faith—a logic of belief, my bulwark all our married life—crumbling a bit. It's the mystery of "Where is God? Is the doctrine of his sovereignty all we have to hold onto?"

Later, Rick visited us with the blessings of prayer, Communion, and conversation. We read together Psalm 124, one of my favorites: "If it hadn't been the Lord who was on our side . . . the flood would have engulfed us, the raging waters would have swept us away. . . . Our help is in the name of the Lord who made heaven and earth." Yes. It's his presence as well as his power that we need.

✳ When Eric came to pray for Harold, he stressed the need for faith that God *has healed* him. Seeing my husband in such daily weakness and increasing distress makes it difficult for me to join in this kind of prayer though H. welcomes it. He feeds on hope more than food. I'm not a Job's comforter, but I think I'm submitting to God in facing the reality of death. Today I bought a dress for a wedding—black with a small floral print and simple styling. Only after getting home did I realize I'd bought a dress equally suitable for a funeral.

Two

Maybe death is a gift, a blessing, a ceasing from struggle and pain, as sleep is. We've been conditioned to think of death as an enemy, but that's because we, the survivors, haven't gone through its doorway, and all we know of it is what's on this side of the door—the loss, separation, grieving. For the one who dies in Christ, it is an opening to a new, unimaginable world of life and light and knowledge. It is, after all, the most natural of all processes. Might not Adam and Eve have died of old age, even without the Fall?

I have seen Harold completing some tasks—getting our wills executed, setting up an active Board for HSP, having the driveway paved, and house painted, imparting financial information to me and the children—these are all death duties. Just as I couldn't sleep last night until Mother's presents were ready for mailing, and the tree decorated, so H. cannot rest until his family *feels* cared for.

✳ Rick's sermon this morning was on the word of God coming upon John the Baptist. The word *epi* (upon), gives the sense of "pouncing upon, with pressure and intensity."

The word *rhema* is to *logos* as laser is to floodlight. This sharp splinter of light from God pierced John (not Tiberius Caesar, or Pontius Pilate, or Herod, or Philip, or Annas, or Caiaphas—the powerful professionals). And it happened in the wilderness, the desert place (not in Rome or Jerusalem). No one likes the desert—sterile and lonely, a rocky barrenness—but it was there, in space and silence, that God was heard and obeyed.

I think of these desert years of mine, not of my choosing. Maybe if it were all smooth and comfortable, if my pride and professionalism were defining life for me, God's steel-quiet, penetrating word would have been lost in the babble and sheen of success.

God, pierce me with your voice. You pierced Mary's heart with misgiving before her Son's death and grief afterwards. But her sorrow and struggle were redemptive—the result, like John the Baptist's, of humility and obedience. If I am destined for the desert, programmed for pain, may my pilgrimage signify something, resolve the impasse between us, produce some lasting result.

Later, Georgia and Bernie prayed for Harold to be at peace no matter what answers God gives—contentment whether he lives or goes to heaven. I felt such relief. This is a hard prayer for me to initiate. I don't want Harold to think I've given up on him or God, or that I view his leaving me with mere resignation. Yet I want us to be able to talk about it and walk it through *together*.

✳ With Terry this morning. We talked about death as a drawing back into self, an inability to retain a sense of *others*. Physical deterioration results in egocentricity. This is my experience of Harold now. He's an adult becoming a child again.

She reminds me that he has his own timetable. I cannot shape his agenda for living or dying. All I can do is watch, and respond.

When I came home I sat on the bed and Harold said, "I've had a rough time." Seems that in the night he'd had some hours of "crystal-clear thinking," and a whole vision of a new Bible study outreach centered around one-on-one discipling. Then, while I was away, his thoughts had "all turned backwards," in terrible confusion, fear, darkness, and doubt, which he thinks was a satanic attack. He cried to God for help. As he told me this, holding my hand, his eyes filled with tears and his face trembled. He cries often and easily these days. I circled him with my arms. He is my little child.

✱ I question if I should go to Grace's wedding, even though I would only be away twenty-four hours. Grace has been like a daughter to us and at least one of us should be there, but there is a wheezing and rattling in Harold's chest that alarms both of us. "I wonder what will happen next," he confesses. When I say, "I'm just happy that your life hasn't been misspent, that you've accomplished so much for God and for other people," he breaks down. "We've done it together. You've been the most wonderful wife—so perfect for me. I love you so much. I can't bear to think of my having to leave you alone." Death is coming more into the open—into our room, our conversation. We both taste its bitterness in our tears.

✱ Anxious about Harold's wheezing, I called Dr. Parker. He arrived, booted and jacketed, dressed for the below-zero weather. "It's a beautiful night!" he announced with his incurable optimism.

Upstairs he visited with us, gentle, taking his time, giving H. a thorough going-over—blood pressure, pulse, lung. When he listened to the lung, its "soft, crackling sound" told him of fluid collecting. Oh, it seems ominous.

"Well, Paul, what I want to know is my prognosis," Harold kept asking. Evading a direct answer, Dr. Parker suggested more frequent use of oxygen, higher calorie intake, lots of fluids. When he mentioned intravenous nutrition, H. rebelled. "That would only prolong this miserable business." That gave me a kind of answer to an earlier question: "How does Harold feel about life-support systems?"

While I was out getting cash for the trip to Washington, D.C. and Grace's wedding, Madeleine called and talked to Harold. This constant reassurance of love and prayers is as good as medicine. I am torn about leaving him, though I've made every preparation for Kris to care for him—potato soup in the refrigerator, lists of all his foods, who to call in case of need. Lay in bed most of the night thinking, thinking, everything turning over and over in my head.

On my return from Grace's wedding, Harold stood up and hugged me strongly as I came into our room. He seemed more alert, responsive, communicative.

And the next morning he rose, dressed, and came down early. A visiting nurse showed up at Dr. Parker's request and took a medical history. (She too can hear the wheezing in the lung.) Medicare covers this service if the patient is homebound but H. declares vigorously he plans to be back at the office next week! Though it's not realistic, it's a relief to see this initiative. Even orneriness is better than passivity!

✻ I told Terry today how *material* I feel, how *un*spiritual. She thinks I have little energy left over after the physical work for the effort of perceiving on a different level. What I'm missing is experience with Christ. He still seems so absent. All the initiative, the ice-breaking seems to lie with me in this Christ-relationship. I feel I must work to get his attention, to bring him down to me. I know that's unbiblical ("the word is near you, even in your mouth"). I know that two thousand years ago Christ did take the initiative; the burden of Incarnation was his. Why then, if he so desires to be one flesh with humans, does he ignore my desire? He must hear me calling. But there's no answer; the silence is deafening. What about "Draw near to God, and he will draw near to you"? When? And is his absence punishment, purgation, discipline?

✱ Elisabeth Elliot phoned at noon, her concern all the more valuable for the unexpectedness of her call. Talking to someone whose husband has died from cancer is unspeakably comforting. No explanations or descriptions are needed. She read to me 2 Corinthians 4:16ff.: "So we do not lose heart. Though our outer nature is wasting away, our inner nature is daily being renewed. For this slight, momentary affliction is preparing for us an eternal weight of glory *out of all proportion* because we look at the unseen rather than the seen, the eternal rather than the transient." I cling to such verses given me by friends.

Harold came into the living room while I was reading those words and asked me to read them again, aloud. After I did we looked into each other's eyes and were able to talk straightforwardly about dying. He told me, "It's not the fact, it's the event that I fear—the unknown, unknowable moment." We cried together. I'm not sorry just for myself. I grieve for him, and for *us*—for the union we've woven of moments and years. Death is tearing at it, will tear it, like a ripped cloth.

Have matted two prints for friends: the burst milkweed pod with seeds and silk silhouetted in light, and the two fallen elderberry leaves caught in the ice the night the temperature dropped. It has been one of my perceptions this year that the beauty of Creation suffuses even decay and death—the *fallen* leaf, the fragile, *shattered* shell of ice, the *frozen* stream, the *burst* pod.

✳ In Dr. Reid's waiting room, Harold said suddenly, loudly, in a near-normal voice, "You'll have to get a stamp made with your signature instead of mine for HSP checks." It was shocking, this announcement of demise. The other people looked embarrassed.

H.'s weight is dropping quickly—fifteen pounds in two weeks. In effect, Dr. Reid said today he could do nothing more for him—radiation would exacerbate his misery, chemo would finish him off. The weight loss shows the cancer's rampant metabolism. Dr. Reid told us to work with Dr. Parker from now on.

So that's that.

✳ Christmas Day. Bright and bitter cold for this day of Incarnation. I took a roll of film of ice crystals on various windows around the house, then prepared a breakfast of eggs, Georgia's special sausage mix, sweet rolls, o.j., coffee, enough to sustain us through the arduous morning task of opening gifts.

In a holiday burst of energy, Harold showered and came down for breakfast. Kris put on "the Messiah." I got the stuffed turkey in the oven and we got down to the business at hand, the presents. John had sent Harold and me an exquisite etching of a Japanese farmhouse under snow. I gave H. a wool fleece mattress cover to ease his hours in bed.

Then I read the first two chapters in Luke aloud, focusing on the repeated appearances of angels, the fear of those who were visited by angels, the repetitions of the words "Fear not!", the perpetual appearance and activity of the Holy Spirit, and the spontaneous way in which people burst into poetry or song!

Tried to reach John by phone and finally got him at the hospital at 4:00 A.M., his time. I was able to get in a few private words with him upstairs and briefed him on his father's condition. Should he come home now? Later? And Jeff was concerned about leaving on his ski trip to France. "Just be *back* as soon as you can," I urged.

In the evening, after Jeff left, I got to work to mount our new cordless phone on the wall by our bed. Marked the place on the wallboard, sawed a chunk of 2x4 to fit the back of the phone exactly, sanded it and affixed the two screws the phone is suspended on, hammered in four long nails at an angle for better grip, smeared wood glue on wall and wood, and hammered the whole thing in place. I didn't hang the phone up on its new bracket because the glue had to set. Throughout this process I was pulled between wanting to do the job myself, to learn, devise, actively solve the tricky little problems, and giving in to H.'s urge to do it himself, or show me how. Should I give him the satisfaction of competence in spite of weakness, or cater to my own need to prove myself to myself? Harold commented with a grin, "You're pretty proficient, aren't you?" "Of course, necessity is the mother of proficiency!" Funny. In the night he woke me and said, "I can't get the phone out of my mind. It's a fixation. Please *hang* the thing." I did, and it stayed up.

✳ Harold is unexpectedly better, sleeping more soundly, full of publishing ideas, eating with more zest, and feeling little pain. Today he wants to go to the Hamlet for lunch! He's drinking, of all things, coffee and root beer!

Kris and I cleared the driveway with the snowblower I

bought Friday night and assembled in the living room, under Harold's watchful eye. She also cleaned out the pantry, and when the Kussros arrived, she baby-sat the girls and made cupcakes while Marian and I went shopping. The children in the house are a wonder and a delight. Lauren offers help constantly. "Can I take Grampa his drink? Can I set the table?" Kate is almost potty-trained and trots off self-importantly to the bathroom by herself at regular intervals. Her wide open eyes match a wide and eager smile. She calls me "Mama" most endearingly. The other side of the coin is that disorder follows them much as a wake follows a ship.

✱ My fifty-seventh birthday—and I've never had such a celebration! Marlene and Jack choreographed a glorious birthday luncheon. The family, the Group, other friends came, bringing exotic foodstuffs—pheasant, cous-cous, spiced German potato salad. Surprisingly, Harold ate heartily. My gifts were half a dozen blooming plants—begonias and hyacinths. I sat and read aloud the loving, perceptive cards accompanying each plant.

With Harold still feeling better, I spent the rest of the day working on the computer—writing letters and doing financial stuff. Made year-end donations, paid bills, filed tax information—the sort of thing that has to be done, but which I detest because I fear making mistakes, or forgetting Something Very Important.

✱ Today I am scheduled to read my poem "Star Song" for the New Year's Day Eucharist at church. Sitting in the sanctuary an hour before the service, I have this quiet, sunlit time in one of my favorite places—a pew next to a window where goblet and loaf are pictured in stained glass above me, the light filtering through. I wish to believe, I *choose* to believe that God is here whether or not I sense him, just as the sunlight penetrates this building through colored glass whether or not I acknowledge it.

Harold will be here, too, for the healing service. Our friends will lay hands on him while Rick prays and anoints him. I wish to believe, I *choose* to believe that there is still hope.

Star Song

We have been having
epiphanies, like suns,
all this year long.
And now, at its close
when the planets
are shining through frost,
light runs like music
in the bones,
and the heart keeps rising
at the sound of any song.
An old magic flows
in the silver calling
of a bell,
rounding
high and clear,
flying, falling,
sounding
the death knell
of our old year,
telling the new appearing
of Christ, our Morning Star.

Now burst,
all our bell throats!

156

Toll, every clapper tongue!
Stun the still night.
Jesus himself gleams through
our high heart notes
(it is no fable).
It is he whose light
glistens in each song sung
and in the true
coming together again
to the stable,
of all of us: shepherds,
sages, his women and men,
common and faithful,
wealthy and wise,
with carillon hearts
and suddenly, stars in our eyes.

157

Three

My recent frost slides are back. They were taken during below-zero temperatures when the frost seems to form faster, in a flash of spreading baroque flourishes across the glass. What heightens the effect of the ice curls and feathers and spears is the brilliant orange of the sun-lightened sky behind them, the color caught and intensified by the crystals, highlighted against the darker, blurred arboreal foreground. Somehow there's an attention-getting incongruity—the remote, enormous incandescence of the sun in service to these small, pale, cold fragments of frost, the permanent illuminating the transient, power caressing fragility, the interplay of far and near kissing on the window before my eyes. This could be a metaphor for God's reaching to humankind to bathe them in brightness . . . or to take them home to heaven.

✳ I'm back sleeping in the blue room. With Harold the nights are so broken. When we were getting ready for bed, he was as frustrated and miserable as I've seen him. Sitting up in his chair, he exploded in a fierce whisper, "I can't *go on* like this. I'm too weak to move, but I'm bored out of my mind and tight as a wire inside. What am I going to do?" All I could do was hug him and hold his hand and tell him I wished I could take it for him. At least in our bed together I was warm; tonight I'm cold and quiet in the blue room with only a defective heating pad for company.

✱ My time with Terry this morning was full of ideas, shifting in and growing clear at the edges. The main one—that God is not outside me, waiting to zap me with his reality once I get my faith in focus, but inside me, part of my own thinking. She thinks I'm like Mary at the Garden Tomb, wanting to touch Jesus. But his reality is greater than the merely tangible. He said to Thomas what he's saying to me: "Blessed are those who do not see or touch me, and who yet believe."

I told her how I miss the physical intimacy with Harold. Sleeping apart from him so I can get the rest I need badly, I'm deprived of the comfort of closeness, and so is he. Even when I lie next to him in bed in the evening, he's too fragile to hug. Last night as he sat in his recliner chair, I bent over him and circled his neck with my arms. "Please love me. I need to feel your love and give you mine." He looked up at me with longing but couldn't move. And I could stay only so long in such a position.

Hearing this, Terry rose, came over to the couch, and hugged me, rocking me in her arms. "You miss the physical Harold, but *this* is how you can feel the presence of Christ—in me and in others who touch you in love." I was so glad to hear, yesterday, that our Marian is coming this weekend. It means more work, and I'm more tired than I can describe, but having another daughter here to hug, to be a companion, will be sweet.

Why was the Incarnation necessary? Because of it, God

could say to us: "I understand you and I know how you feel." But then he came closer still, in the Holy Spirit by whom he impregnated Mary with the physical seed of Christ; and by whom he now impregnates us with the spiritual reality of Christ, who is being formed in us almost as a fetus is formed in the womb. This is why we can say we have the mind of Christ. But we're not just acted upon; we participate in what happens.

✱ Our nephew Larry called, suggesting that he come and visit Harold. I'm realizing how remote all the Shaw family must feel, so far away in New England. They call often, and want to see Harold, but are hesitant to add to our stress.

Paul Shaw has been here since Monday. Paul has kept urging Harold to exercise more, as if by will power he could regain his muscle tone and vigor. (It's the classic misinterpretation of the sick by the healthy—I have done it often myself—that wellness is a matter of choice and decision.) On Wednesday, incredibly, H. did manage to get dressed, come downstairs, and drive with Paul and me to the office, where he showed his brother around, proudly, but very slowly and shakily, walking behind me and leaning heavily, with a hand on each of my shoulders for support, pausing every few steps to rest or sit down.

✱ The last two days have been the most difficult of the past year. Harold's lung seems full of mucus which rattles loudly with each breath. Most of the time he coughs fruitlessly, producing nothing for all his effort. He's eaten little today. A strong pain in his side keeps him from lying prone, so he sits in his reclining chair, getting what rest he can in that position.

I slept restlessly in Kris's room with Lauren, as Marian and

Karl came in from Indianapolis yesterday and stayed the night, sleeping in the blue room. I got up several times to check on Harold, fearing he'd choke in his sleep. I cannot imagine that he can go on like this for long. I see my dearest shrinking, pulling away from me.

Rather than try to escape from this trauma or distract myself in an effort to ease or forget it, I am trying a new tactic—welcoming the pain, receiving it, letting it penetrate in an almost surgical way to do its work without the dulling of anesthesia. It feels more therapeutic, and I'm not playing mind games this way. Is it masochistic? It might be, if the pain were self-inflicted. But the agony of parting and death is inescapable, part of the human condition. James says, "Count it all joy, brothers, when you undergo trials, for you know that the testing of your faith produces steadfastness." Pain has a work to do in our refinement so that our gold is not adulterated.

✻ As I came home from getting mail at the office at noon, sleet filled the air and bounced off the windshield, then turned to large, soft flakes that began to fall so thickly that in minutes they were piled inches deep on the road, coating every stone and branch. The landscape became a monochrome patterned with intricate blacks and grays against the matte white. The few splashes of color that remained—the solitary diamond of the yellow road sign, the jewel of the flashing red light at North and Fair Oaks, the clusters of scarlet high-bush cranberries—achieved an astonishing brilliance.

Then, just as suddenly as it began, the snow shower stopped, the air cleared, and the gray sky turned all pearly, full of pink light so luminous, like the inside of a shell, that even the snow-piled branches showed dark against it.

✳ Marian is pregnant again. Kris was pleased to have heard the news *before me*! This is a day of love and closeness, in spite of Harold's growing weakness. At church I grasped at the words from Nehemiah 8:9–10: "Do not mourn or weep . . . Do not be grieved, for the joy of the Lord is your strength."

✳ From HSP Steve called to tell us that in devotions they had a special hour of prayer for H. and me. God is speaking to me through the concern of my friends. I don't see direct answers to either their prayers or my own. But maybe their love and concern in itself is a demonstration of comfort from God.

And Steve's visit to Harold perked him up a bit this afternoon. Then Jeff arrived back from France—an added encouragement. I brought our dinner up to the bedroom, and the four of us ate together (though H. took very little). Jeff lay across our bed after supper and told his father and me all about his trip. I spent the night back in our bed, with Harold sedated with codeine, Tylenol, and aspirin, in the recliner across the room from me. I felt easier, being close to him. He's on three liters of oxygen an hour all the time now.

✳ As John urged me to do, I've been talking with Harold about dying, and fixing his thinking on heaven and Christ rather than on his pain and struggle. We've had several letters suggesting how a Christian dies. One mentioned 2 Corinthians 4:7–12: "We have this treasure in jars of clay to show that this all-surpassing power is from God and not from us. We are hard pressed on every side, but not crushed; perplexed, but not in despair; persecuted, but not abandoned; struck down, but not destroyed. We always carry around in our body the death of Jesus, so that the life of Jesus may also be revealed in our body. For we who are alive are always given over to death for Jesus' sake, so that his life may be revealed in our mortal body. So then, death is at work in us, but life is at work in you."

✳ Dr. Parker has come in response to my concern about Harold's increasing struggle with breathing. After listening to the lung, Dr. P. says soberly, "I think we'd better put in that call to John."

With the Red Cross initiating the Emergency Leave, once again I call Harold's sister, Marion Borg, in Massachusetts, urging her to come right away. Marion says, in incredulous tears, "I can't believe it. It's really happening, isn't it?"

Next come the young men from the hospital supply to set up an electric bed in our bedroom. Harold refuses to attempt the move until Kay, the visiting nurse, arrives at noon. She is chubby, loud, and cheerful, telling him he is so cute and so young-looking for his age. At first I resent her brashness but he seems to rally for her, relieved perhaps, that someone is acting normally. She takes some time instructing me in how to give shots of Demerol for pain, stabbing an orange in demonstration. But strangely, Harold's pain ebbs.

We sit together most of the afternoon, my hand supporting his bowed head, his body curled forward as his mother's had in her wheelchair before her death. At one point I find he has put his arm under my elbow to support *me*.

The afternoon goes by in whispered conversation. I tell him how much I love him, what a wonderful husband he has been, how well and thoroughly I have felt loved and cherished by him. I ask his forgiveness for my moods, my failings. "What moods, what failings?" he asks. And over and over again, the words, "I love you."

By the time Kris comes home from school, he has grown clammy and damp. She sits by his bed and cries into his hand, kisses his pale head, tells him how she loves him, hears him tell his love for her.

At six o'clock Eric arrives to pray for Harold—a long, last prayer of committal, the hope of physical healing relinquished. When Jeff comes in from Chicago, he and Kris hold Harold's hands while I warm rolls and casserole in the oven and bring the food upstairs to be near Harold. But none of us is hungry. H. recognizes Chuck and Winnie Christensen when they drop by about eight, but he can't speak. Eyes half-closed, his meager energy is poured into maintaining the rhythm of his breathing.

As Chuck reads Scripture, Harold's breath seems to falter. For about thirty seconds his chest stops heaving. Suddenly I realize that the hiss of oxygen through his nasal cannula has stopped. The silence is uncanny. In my intense scrutiny of Harold, I have forgotten to keep track of the oxygen level so I can switch to the other tank. Leaping up, I quickly turn on the other valve to restore the flow. It is a dreadful moment. Kris sobs and cries out. Jeff holds me close. In that instant death reaches out and touches us unmistakably.

Have I done Harold a favor, turning the oxygen on again? Should this have been the end? His breathing starts again, but he is comatose, hands slack and blue, skin icy, pupils unseeing.

Soon after Chuck leaves for the airport to fetch Marion Borg and Royal. Paul Parker administers one last injection, and the coma deepens. It is in this state that Karen and David find us.

While Karen is reading 2 Corinthians 4, Harold's breathing slows, so light and slight that it is almost imperceptible. It is difficult to know when it finally stops.

My darling lies there, waxy pale, his skin gleaming in the light like a tallow candle, his nose sharp, his forehead shining with cold sweat. We wait, maybe five or six minutes. When we are sure, I rise slowly, and turn off the oxygen.

"Go in peace, Harold," I say huskily. "Be at peace."

I feel detached, amputated, flat, numb with tears that will not come.

THE TREE
AND THE SOD

February–May 1986

Your death blows a strange bugle call,
*   friend, and all is hard*
To see plainly or record truly. The new
*   light imposes change,*
Readjusts all a life-landscape as it thrusts
*   down its probe from the sky,*
To create shadows, to reveal waters, to
*   erect hills and deepen glens.*
The slant alters. I can't see the old
*   contours . . .*
Is it the first sting of the great winter, the
*   world-waning? Or the cold of spring?*
A hard question and worth talking a
*   whole night on. But with whom?*
Of whom now can I ask guidance? With
*   what friend concerning your death*
Is it worth while to exchange thoughts
*   unless—oh unless it were you?*

—C. S. LEWIS, **To Charles Williams**

One
───────────────────────────

I keep looking back at these recent days, wondering. Unreality wraps them round like a tent. It encloses me in an artificial darkness. Unlike the sky, there is no twilight; I see no pinprick stars. The hymns and Scriptures we have chosen for the funeral seem fitting, but somehow abstract.

I am a widow, a social symbol, my face smiling to the family, my friends, with a sharp superficial brightness that glares like an unshielded light bulb. I am alone, but I cannot cry. Where is God when I need him? Harold's body lies in the casket, but there's no warmth in it. He isn't there for me, his real presence has flown. The tent closes in, a smothering tarpaulin, a bodysack. I am feeling buried alive in my own emotional emptiness.

I keep asking myself, unbelieving, "How can this huge, irreversible, dreaded thing have happened to my lover and to me?" Yet I don't act very differently. I dress, eat, drive the car, shop, write letters, am the same person, and yet everything is washed with the pallor of gray. A wide, indefinable sadness surrounds but doesn't quite reach me. With family and children in the house, the noise level drowns out the silence that would allow me to think and feel.

✳ Everyone said the funeral service on Monday was beautiful—the Eucharist celebrated in the nave of Trinity Episcopal in Wheaton, with its uninterrupted space lit with white candles, the congregation of friends filling the pews. Sitting as I was in the front row with Robin, Marian, John, Jeff, and Kris, I couldn't see everyone, but the back of my head could feel their eyes. Megs' reading of 2 Corinthians 4—human, earthy, but eloquent; "The King of Love My Sheperd Is"—Psalm 23 set to music; Rick's homily, which likened Harold to a seed sown in the ground awaiting resurrection, to sprout in heavenly leaves and fruit, like the "instant gardens" of the Bedouins. After these words, we sang, "Praise, My Soul, the King of Heaven" (my lips moving, but my soul feeling remote, unmoved). Then all the family and I went to the altar and took the Eucharist, followed by my many friends streaming forward to partake of Christ's body and blood. Some touched my hand or bent to embrace me on their way back to their pews. Was that how God showed me his presence?

My unnatural calmness held until Myrna White began to sing from the balcony:

> Neither life nor death shall ever
> From the Lord his children sever.
> Unto them his grace he showeth
> And their sorrows all he knoweth.
>
> Though he giveth or he taketh,
> God his children ne'er forsaketh.
> 'Tis his loving purpose solely
> To preserve them, pure and holy.

Then, caught in a flame of emotion, I began to weep. My heart felt hollow, drawn out of me, crushed and burned like incense.

Leading my children, I followed the casket and the eight pallbearers to the back of the church and outside. The drive to

Bronswood was long, but the graveside ceremony in a cold, damp wind, was mercifully brief. The unreality persisted. This was my husband whom I was leaving under the gray sky. Or was it? Where was he? I was too numb and gray myself to know. John and Leslie, cousins and longtime friends, started the hymn "Through the love of God our Savior, all will be well." I wanted to believe it.

✱ The day after the funeral I came down with flu but got out of bed to see Terry today. I described to her my lack of emotion: Why am I not feeling more pain or the grief of Harold's departure? She thinks I have been grieving all year, preparing for death, learning to accept the inevitable separation.

I feel separated from God too. I want more than anything else to know he's on my side, yet because I can't rationally, finally prove his existence, I fear the risk of faith, the climbing out on a divine limb, for fear of being deceived and finding only an emptiness in which I am an accidental collection of atoms.

As I once told Terry, I've always felt that such doubt as mine was condemned in James 1, that because I doubt I'm therefore damned as double-minded. Terry views the words "Let him ask in faith, nothing doubting," not as condemnation but as God's desire for us to win all the rewards of faith and not exclude ourselves from God's blessing.

She asked me what I would do with the rest of my life if I were convinced God did not exist. I said, "Probably self-destruct." "But what about all your epiphanies, your moments of beauty? Aren't they enough to give you a reason to live?" "No, because they'd have no value without a God to give them meaning." As I think back, I believe I was exaggerating—that I would keep going just to snatch what beauty and pleasure and meaning I could from the natural world.

I don't understand myself. Integrity. It implies integration, wholeness, centeredness. But I feel split, instead, between belief and unbelief, or believing given truth and making it my own. The conformist sheathing the non-conformist—both elements I find in myself in equal proportions.

A poem sent by Madeleine seems an answer to my confusion:

Observe and Contemplate

> Observe and contemplate,
> make real, bring to be.
> Because we note the falling tree
> the sound is truly heard.
> Look! The sunrise! Wait—
> it needs us to look, to see,
> to hear, and speak the word.
>
> Observe and contemplate
> the cosmos and our little earth.
> Observing, we affirm the worth
> of sun and stars and light unfurled.
> So let us, seeing, celebrate
> the glory of Love's incarnate birth
> And sing its joy to all the world.
>
> Observe and contemplate,
> make real. Affirm. Say Yes,
> And in this season sing and bless
> wind, ice, snow; rabbit and bird;
> Comet and quark; things small and great,
> oh, observe and joyfully confess
> The birth of Love's most lovely Word!

✳ Scores and scores of letters are coming in. I am not really astounded at the esteem in which Harold was held; I was just in ignorance of much of it.

Today a letter from Maxine arrived with a poem, "For Luci, Now" which takes my image of the "rusty trellis supporting the thorned rose" and extends it. And then I did cry. The poem penetrated and turned its point in me.

A letter from Madeleine written on January 30 while on the high seas, astonished me.

> Oh, Luci, dear Luci:
> Friday morning early I was sitting on the deck of the freighter on which Hugh and I were traveling, and writing in my journal. Suddenly I was assailed by a great wave of grief. Hugh, seeing me, said, "What's the matter?" "I don't know." "You look as though you're about to cry." "Yes." "Why?" "I don't know." But the sadness was intense. Now I know why. Marilyn had left urgent messages for me to call, so I did, last night, when we got home around ten o'clock. As I dialed her number I knew what the message was going to be. She told me that Harold died Thursday night.

It seems that my dear friends are really bearing my burden with me in ways that transcend the rational. Perhaps I feel so little pain because it's being borne by them?

✳ The sense of strangeness blankets me still. I'm following my normal Sunday pattern and need to remind myself that this Sunday is different, that even my house and its contents are changing. At my request, Paul took some of Harold's suits and jackets; Mark, some shoes; and all the children claimed some of

171

their father's shirts, socks, ties, sweaters. I washed and bleached all his handkerchiefs this afternoon—for what? He won't ever use them. He's gone. He doesn't live here any more, though his name at this address is still on checks, credit cards, legal papers, and on many of the letters that I find in the mailbox, which still bears the name "Harold Shaw" along its backbone. I am caught between wanting to retain these evidences of his past reality and presence in this place, and needing to acknowledge the current truth: He is not here; he has gone.

This afternoon John and I went to see "Out of Africa." The beauty of the country, the timelessness of its landscape, and the art of the film bound me like a spell. Caught in the picture, I remembered how I'd hoped to see the film with Harold, to be part of it together. The implacability of our separation was like a sudden blow in the face. I sobbed and sobbed, messily, with no tissues at hand, John trying in vain to comfort me.

But it was pure relief to cry, at last to begin to feel and know the depth of my missing him, that I am a real person with real grief about real bereavement.

Music, poetry, film, break through to me. Perhaps that is why art has value—to plunge us back into our own reality. And where is God in all of this? I'm not quite sure. Perhaps I just haven't recognized him.

✳ I cleaned out Harold's drawer on the left of our bathroom sink today—the thin petals of old, saved soap, the worn combs with his fine hair still woven into them, the shoe polishing cloth that said "The Portman Hotel, London," Mylanta tablets crackling in their clear plastic sleeves, nail files with the marks of his nails still on them. Now the drawer is all clean and neat, the dust of his skin cells and nail clippings, gone. And I'm sorry I did it.

No more. There will be no more long car trips—he driving,

me knitting or writing; no more reading aloud to him, no more early-morning oatmeal or all-bran with banana slices eaten in the breakfast room; no more cutting the long, sweet summer grass, or sitting together on the back deck while the sun falls behind the trees and the fireflies dance and twinkle into life in the dusk; no more companionable Cape Cod holidays, or walks hand-in-hand along our familiar country roads, or cooperative vegetable gardening, or excursions to Al's Ice Creamery in St. Charles. No more snaking out new back routes for shortcuts; no more antiques, or garage sales Saturday mornings, or Artist Series concerts, or waking at midnight to bounce book ideas off each other. No more praying together for our kids. No more kneeling side by side at the Communion rail. No more warm closeness in bed on winter nights in our flannel nightshirts, secure against the chill of the outside world. No more lovemaking and aftersleep. No more.

✱ Karen asked me if I felt all right about our Group having a memorial evening for Harold. I said, "Yes. I want that. And I want it to be hard." I want those feelings of grief to have their way with me, so that I'll know I'm all there as the pain presses in.

I want to read to the Group some of my poems about sickness and separateness. To read them aloud to my friends of the heart may undam the silent reservoir in me. I hope I may cry and cry.

The Separation

No matter how intense
our touching,
or how tender—heads
burrowing fiercely

173

into chests, or fingers
sure, silken—
there are no
contiguous nerves
to bridge
our bodies' gaps, no
paths of words
to join our souls.
Though each images
the other's pain or
pleasure, two
remain two.
We have been seamed,
not grafted. Though
our steps interlock,
each dances
his own dance.

Do you read into this
a strategy:
separation for
survival's sake?
See it, rather,
as predicament—
our world's ache
to be joined,
to know
and be known.

✳ When I go out, even briefly, swathed in scarves, the zero
cold catches me in the throat. The cold also intensifies the
aloneness. Both are so penetrating, so chilly. And the light still
dies away into darkness so early in the afternoon.

174

I found an old fifty-dollar traveler's check, unused. Took it to the bank and asked the teller what I should do with it. When I explained that Harold had died recently, she looked astonished. "He died?" she asked. "I didn't know," and burst into tears. She'd known him well for years. "Sorry to upset you," she said. "I'm just so shocked. He was such a lovely man."

✱ I filled out one of many forms today. None of the three choices—"single," "married," "divorced," fits me. Decided "single" comes closest. To be a single woman again after 32 1/2 years of marriage is an astonishing thought. "Married" means safe, comfortable, stable, loved, protected in some indefinable way.

I'm glad, though, that my single state is a result of death, not divorce, which carries with it a freight of bitterness and anger and psychic pain. My separation from Harold is clean-cut, with no breaks, no regret or remorse about unfaithfulness or disloyalty or neglect. I know he loved me wholly, as I loved him.

Death has sealed off those married years like a capped bottle of perfume. Our marriage cannot be lost or shattered. Nothing can touch it now. It's safe—one of my treasures laid up in heaven where no mothy resentment or rusty dissolution can erode it. In a sense our marriage was like a flower that matured into a fruit, sweet and wholesome, and I am like a seed dropped from that mature fruit, now withered and dead. I am the result of a long relationship and I want to fall in good ground and produce more fruit—of what kind God and I will have to determine.

Two

Today, ten days after the funeral, our dead oak tree came down. Long-ago lightning had sheared off its top and split its trunk down the middle. Then rot had deepened the central deadness until the leaves each succeeding summer showed more sparse and sickly, and last year it produced no leaves at all. Raccoons have lived in it, their little patchwork faces peering over the ragged top of the trunk at dusk, a few feet from Kris's bedroom window.

With the temperature not budging above zero, the ground is adamantine with frost. Bernie and his friend Jim and their sons came over with saws and ropes and climbing gear and brought down the tree, piece by piece, until at last the main trunk was severed at the root. It fell with a mighty *thunk* that shook the house.

Tonight, when I came home, the fire they had built in the rot-hollowed root was still glowing, burning deep into the ground. It's painful to witness the fall of such a giant, to see it treated with such indignity after all those solid years of growth, just as it's hard to see a good man shrivel into a helpless shell, laid out by human hands and disposed of.

That everything adjusts and smooths out and keeps on going as if nothing has happened seems like an insult to the grandness of a tree or a man. "And the place thereof shall know it no more." Ichabod. Damn.

* My sense of blankness and numbness was enormous during Communion. I was saying all the words, performing the actions, with no sense of any reality behind them. Weeping, with disappointment and loneliness in the pew after coming down from the altar rail, I sobbed harder when next to me a friend put her warm hand and arm across my shoulders and around my neck. Still, pain poured out of me along with my tears.

* Yesterday the sun shone after nearly a week of fog, sleet, snow, and assorted glooms. Bernie and Greg Bosch finished up the business of the tree Saturday, splitting the few remaining chunks of usable wood and loading them onto their truck, digging the ashes and stones out of the concavity of last weekend's fire, raking up the sawdust and twigs into a new blaze. Within twenty-four hours, after the fire had burned down to a bowl of pale new ash and a tendril of smoke, the visible rim of the original tree showing above the verge of grass had been eaten away. You would hardly know that a tree had been there, though its invisible shape, the vertical out-branching space it had filled in the air, still remains in my mind, and its roots still exist in some subterranean place—like Harold, whose unseen force still pervades my life and thinking, even though his visible presence is gone.

✱ The Group met at the Mains' to share their memories of Harold, and I read my poem "Spice" and Maxine's follow-up poem, with the image of the rusty trellis being replaced by an invisible trellis of grace. When David asked me how the Group could best support me, I told them they had done it for the last sixteen months, and were still doing it, but I asked them not to shield me from pain, which I need to feel more cleanly.

"One of the traits of strong families," David said, "is that they don't fall apart in crisis. Another is the sense of continuity with past and future generations." He told of an African tribe who count the recently dead and the about-to-be-born as integral to their population. I thought of our own life cycle—of Harold, and of Marian's unborn baby.

✱ I clean my teeth in the morning, squeezing toothpaste from the last tube that H. bought and used. The incongruity strikes me again—that the plastic tube is here, and he is gone. The cake of Pear's soap we shared in the shower is thinning to transparency with use.

I felt desperately lonely this afternoon, missing Harold. Like listening for a diminishing echo I find it hard, already, to recall his voice, the feel of him, his essence. In the bedroom recliner chair where he spent so much time those last weeks, I sat with my elbows pushed into its corners and tried to imagine his arms around me. It didn't work; the cool touch of the velour was impersonal; it only accentuated the fact of his absence. Perhaps it is a reaching for fantasy, an untruth, for me to want to feel him here when he's not.

I derive some comfort in the long, solitary stretches of night silence from holding or hugging Harold's square, knitted "head thing" (as we all called it) which still lies like a miniature blanket, folded under his pillow. I knitted it for him years ago to cover his head and prevent headaches from the cold night air. It still imparts such a unique sense of him. And yet these reminders, so comforting in one way, are painful in another, as is his Swiss hiking stick (with which he supported himself when he was at his weakest), still hanging from the bookshelf where he put it last, and his well-marked Bible which he read so constantly. These emblems of Harold, visible, tangible, there where I see them every day, tell me more strongly than words that he is now invisible, intangible.

Gerald Brenan, in *Thoughts in a Dry Season,* writes: "The great thing about marriage is that it enables one to be alone without feeling loneliness." Widowhood proves the converse— even when we're not alone, we feel lonely at the core. Bereavement, death, is radical surgery on a marriage. Now the anesthesia is beginning to wear off. The nerves tingle, the pain reflexes twitch. I am beginning to feel the rawness of amputation.

✱ I'm taking the course to be licensed as a Lay Reader. I find some penetrating ideas in one of my textbooks. In its broadest sense, worship "assigns value," not only the absolute value of God but the relative value we place on everything else. I read: "After we have responded to God in Christ as the ultimate or absolute in an act of worship, we go on to ascribe . . . value to the persons and things we encounter in the ordinary course of life, using the criterion provided by our meeting with the holy. For Christians, that is the love of God revealed in Jesus Christ . . ." Yes. Perceiving God's love and holiness made me more appreciative of these same values in a human—Harold.

I realize that in one important sense I haven't lost him. A letter from Elisabeth Elliot yesterday quoted Amy Carmichael: "All that was ever ours is ours forever," which reinforces my sense that all the great good and joy of our marriage is inviolable now.

Madeleine called this morning. I've been on her mind. Once again, the "allrightness" of Harold's death—a Christian death at peace with God, friends, family—became apparent by contrast with the death of a young ballet dancer M. knew who had committed suicide after involvement in the occult. I told Madeleine about the oak tree—its dying, its removal—and it became clear to me as I talked that the wound in the sod, with the roots of the tree still smoldering deep under the surface, is me—all raw, fevered with fire, and unhealed yet. I have to wait for the sod to grow back.

Three

Driving to church today with Kris, I felt the lifting of the pall of frost. The air is rowdy with wind from the south. A chickadee whistles her spring song over and over—"Phoebe, Phoebe." Elizabeth Rooney, who was here Friday night, says that spring arrives in stages—the spring of light, the spring of running water, the spring of green. We've begun to feel our spirits lightened by the spring of light, as the nights shrink at the edges, and the days stretch out, taking over, gathering new minutes at each end. Maybe now the spring of running water is at hand.

* There's a bittersweetness about all these days. Calls from my brother, my sons, my friends, make me realize how much I need a full, unequivocal relationship to fill this season with reciprocal human response as well as beauty. I resent doubts, hesitations, reservations, limited times with those I love. What I want is three-dimensional, permanent. I know what I really want—Harold.

I find I'm longing for his approval, his "well done" at new advances I'm making, progress in this new adventure. I need affirmation. I miss his warm guarantees that what I'm doing is done well: "That's it, Lu! You did it! You hit the nail on the head!" Without him I lack security. There's freedom, of course, in having no one but myself to consult, but it's a bleak benefit. Ingrid Trobisch says that "grief is the price of loving."

✳ The two factors that seem to redeem life from despair are relationships and meaningful work to do. Yesterday I had a call from Regent College, inviting me to teach poetry at their three-week summer session. Amazing how such a prospect gave color to my day!

✳ On the drive to church I played the King's College Choir Easter tape. One phrase that rang into my head from the epistle was "alive to God." With sun-roof open, and light, and live air filling the landscape, I felt that this is what I want to be—not only alive and open to God's world but to *him.*

In church I sat with David and Karen. I saw Karen's hand reach out and hold David's and throbbed with the deprivation of all that holding hands means—caring, tenderness, closeness, comfort. I miss a man's hug. When Jeff hugged me hard yesterday it met such a deep need in me—but for so brief a time.

It's not just Harold I miss, though that is so central a lack that I ache with it at my core, but the whole way of life we'd built together—things like having guests for Sunday noon dinner after church, so often a roast of beef, with gravy and Yorkshire pudding. Haven't had that sort of meal for months now.

✽ I started the day with a fast mile walk. The grass, faintly tinged on the sunny slopes with green, glittered in the melting frost. The air was intoxicatingly fresh. Exhilaration! The idea of my being "dead to sin and alive to God" expanded consciously in my imagination. The air was perfectly still so that the calls and songs of robins and phoebes formed a web of clear sounds all around me as I walked, not muffled or blown away by the strong, gusty winds of the days earlier this week. I took my accustomed circuit, finishing up with the curlicue into Wayne Oaks Lane and our driveway. All the way the edges of the turf, the sun-warmed banks and sheltered spots, were brightening with green—spears of grass pushing up through dead, pale straw, and I felt my kinship with the sod.

From my reading in *Song of Solomon* this morning:

> My lover spoke and said to me
> "Arise my darling, my beautiful one, and come
>   with me.
> See, the winter is past; the rains are over and
>   gone.
> Flowers appear on the earth. The season of
>   singing has come.
> Now birdsong is heard in our land."

✽ At the Good Friday service—a continuation of Holy Thursday, beginning and ending in silent prayer—I knelt with the congregation, then moved with a group to the altar to view and meditate on the cross. Rick had pointed out that the Old Testament sacrifices, during which each failing individual presented an animal for slaughter and watched the gush of blood as its throat was cut and its body burned on the high altar, was meant to induce repentance and healthy guilt in the sacrificer, and thankfulness that a substitute was suffering for his failures.

Yet somehow we see Christ's death, an almost exact parallel, at a remove. The elapsed time, the culture gap, the accretion of tradition and ritualistic repetition distances us from the real fact of the crucifixion and from the personal, human suffering of Jesus. In an effort to restore this immediacy, even to allow us to participate in the event itself, Rick leaned a St. Damien's cross against the altar as a focus for our meditation.

I am troubled that in me such repetitions seem to blunt rather than sharpen this sense of reality. This must be where my faith, the eye of the imagination centered in my soul, must learn to penetrate in a focused way. Trivial distractions (the off-key high note from someone in the choir, the color of my neighbor's tie) seduce my thinking so that I may actually wing through the Eucharistic prayer, may even take bread and wine into my mouth and cross myself, but my mind flits around like Noah's dove above the waters, unable to find a place to land and rest. Sacramental thinking suggests that grace is imparted in the elements whether or not we are conscious of the process. I take some comfort in that. I must believe it is God's intention to bless, to bypass my inattention in his mercy, knowing that I am dust.

✱ The Easter Vigil. The luggage is in the car, ready for our flight south. The service started in total darkness, then a brazier with incense was lit and the Paschal candle passed the flame to the small candles in the hands of the participants. Three baptisms, during which we all renewed our baptismal vows. I felt a flick of water cold on my hand as Rick sprinkled the congregation. The light grew stronger through the stained glass. At Communion I went to the altar in tears at the thought of Resurrection (Christ's and ours, mine and Harold's). Cried freely there, and Rick squeezed my hand as he placed the crumb of bread in my palm.

After embracing Karen, Jack, and Marlene in the aisle, I made a quick exit through the undercroft. It was well worth the early rise to feel the completion of Lent and Holy Week on this dawning Easter day.

✱ Sunrise at Sanibel. Kris and I are in the D'Arcys' condominium again. I am thinking of our Florida trip with Harold last February—not perfect, because of his weakness and lassitude, but a time of release from winter. My few times of freedom, walking alone, photographing, seemed more precious for their brevity and rarity. This time I am really free; all the time is mine, but the sparkle has gone out of it.

I'd hoped that coming here would revive my memories of how Harold was when we were last here—not healthy, but well enough for us to sleep together, walk on the beach, drive to Captiva, eat out. But I'm finding it almost impossible to see Harold as he was BC—Before Cancer—hale and hearty, companionable, decisive, warm, loving, real. In one way I don't want to lose the sense of loss, the blank feeling of strangeness, because it is all I have left of him.

✱ A long early walk, a circuit along Gulf Drive to the beach access and then back along the shore. The last two days a strong, offshore wind has blown in and the surf is high. I walk along the arcs of waves, avoiding the foam as it reaches for my sneakers. I note how much prettier the shells are when wet; not only does the sun catch them and gleam from them, but the color is intensified. It's easier to find and glean the bright colors where the waves are washing the spread of shells because the whites are whiter and the reds, pinks, purples, oranges, are more intense. Perhaps, in the same way, crisis, trouble, stress— the breakers in our lives—show us up truly for who we are.

✳ I had an encounter with a family at the condominium pool yesterday—two young parents with their three little children. I don't even know their names, but he's a surgeon who trained in Chicago. I mentioned to the woman that I'd lost my husband two months ago, and that serious, concerned look that comes in response to such a comment flew into her pretty, tanned face. Later she came to the pool with a book for me, *The Grieving Time,* by a woman whose husband died of cancer at sixty-four—a journal-type book. I finished it in half-an-hour, but it gave me the author, a fellow-widow, to cry with. So many of her feelings and insights are exactly mine.

Sarah (I asked her name later) sat and talked with me for a while; she and her husband have recently lost a close friend and she is raw and tender from it still. Her concern and sympathy opened me up to my own feelings and I cried on and off all afternoon, for myself, for her, for the company of the bereaved. It is unusual for a stranger to deliberately leave her lounge chair at the pool and come over to talk to me, a widow, so easily shunned or ignored, with sensitivity and compassion and understanding.

✳ Kris and I have had a confrontation. It seems as if, when I come into a room, she leaves, that her eyes are veiled to me, that there are no ways for us to reach each other's hearts. I asked if I were irritating her, or doing something that made her feel sad. She just said, "No, it's not your fault. It's mine." She was downcast the rest of the afternoon. Since then I've prayed for her often, for comfort, for words and ways to release her pain. She, too, was here with Harold last year. She feels it.

I am so inadequate with Kris. Alone—together in the same space but each alone—neither our words nor actions intersect. I dreaded eating out at a restaurant last night, wondering how to fill the time waiting for our meal to be served, since conversation with her tends to be sparse and factual: "How is your reading coming? Tell me what you're going to write in your paper. Where would you like to eat tomorrow night?" "Fine. I don't know. I don't care."

But it was easier than I'd anticipated. We talked about Max and Sarah—the doctor and his wife—and about *Jane Eyre.* Kris is looking for color symbolism in the developing plot and came up with some interesting samples. I wish I could lead in to a more personal dialogue: "What color symbolism marks your feelings?" But as soon as I approach something so intimate, I get anxious and stumble over my words. They come out all wrong and I feel dumb, a self-evaluation which she confirms by the way she looks at me. What does she really want, or need? Should I give her more time? Trust her to find her own way? Trust the Spirit to do what I cannot? This uncertainty is the hardest thing I bear right now.

✱ Kris had to get back to school and left yesterday on a 7:00 A.M. flight. I fear the solitude with no one to talk to, to dine with in the evenings. Last night I ventured into the "Mad Hatter" and saw a woman eating alone. I thought, "If she can do it, so can I."

This is the first true challenge of being solitary for me. The old truism about "pain shared is halved and pleasure shared is doubled" is coming back to me, not flat and theoretical, but sharp and shaped like life. The fear of being alone is a weight, a drag on my spirit. I feel faintly nauseated at the prospect of dinner, though I've had little food all day. The only way to learn to be alone is *to be alone.*

Still, I miss human voices, and tune the FM radio to classical music to break the hush. In this tastefully and comfortably furnished place, with its plush white carpets, I pad around and cannot even hear my own footfalls. I feel disembodied, like the resident ghost.

In the night I dreamed of H. for the first time since his death. He had come to pick me up at the airport. After reaching the car in the parking lot, he handed me the keys and said, "You drive," then got into the back seat. It felt so freeing, like getting his permission to take the driver's seat in my life.

✳ My walk this morning brought me back along the beach east to west. A high wind was blowing, throwing heavy waves at the beach and eating away at the slope of sand and shells. It has taken the beach out from under our wooden walkway and steps, undercutting them by several feet.

I love the way the sea-grapes grow, each leaf a joining of two flattened circles to a central rib. The new buds push out first as a glossy lime green, then, unfolding, enlarging, burnish into copper and finally a fiery red—losing the sheen with time, but gaining color—a parable of youth and age?

I am *alive,* and the magnificence of this created universe surrounds me. What I must learn to discern in its impersonal forces and phenomena is the Spirit, not only brooding upon the face of the waters, but coming closer—residing in me, linking me to my Creator and through him to other created beings.

Four

A weight of worry sits on my chest. Kris. Her latest crisis seems to revolve around not being invited to the Junior-Senior banquet by a certain young man. And I know I must talk to her about this coming weekend. After a birthday party, she'll be staying overnight with Jeff downtown. I must also alert her to my concerns—the possible dangers of drugs, drinking, sex, cynicism, the lack of the sort of basic values I wish for her. At least she must be cautioned, not taken by surprise. Nor do I want to alienate her from her brother, who really cares for her. It's just that Jeff's ideas about what constitutes a "good experience" may differ from mine.

I feel so lacking in wisdom. I'm feeling keenly the blank where Harold isn't. I'm not sure he would have all the answers either, but at least in talking together we might arrive at a clearer conclusion. I stood in the closet and cried, "Oh, honey, I miss you so much! And I can't *tell* you I miss you. And you're not here to counsel and console me as you always did when I was down!"

I've been thinking, too, about how hard relinquishment must have been for Harold before he died. To know that your wife and children must go on living and you can't share the moments of joy, the triumphs, nor be there to steady them in the difficult times; not to know whom your sons and your youngest daughter will marry, or how their lives turn out; to give up your own life's work—leave it all hanging; to have to trust that your mate will make good decisions, knowing all the time that she'll make mistakes and have to pay for them alone—it must have wrenched at him. And I'm only now realizing it. How uncomplaining he was about all this. How uncomprehending I was about the emotional pain he must have suffered.

All of which points me again to my heavenly Parent. Like Kris, I struggle with questions and rebel at certain perceptions. Does God minutely plan and coordinate his children's lives? We second-guess God, assigning to him motives and purposes which are merely our interpretations of our human circumstances. How do I interpret the accidental burning of a friend's cabin, for example? Was God in charge, or on vacation? Did he "allow it" for some inscrutable purpose? And do celestial powers really concern themselves with human minutiae?

We assume God to be good and powerful and fair, and so we have to translate his actions, or lack of them, in terms that don't disturb such theological assumptions. We always give God a loophole. When things go smoothly and life is a series of triumphs, we thank the Almighty for our good fortune, as if it were a plan specially devised for us by him. And when, by cancer, or poverty, or famine, or war, we are devastated, we still thank him, asserting through our tears that he has a reason for it all, somewhere. But are we only pawns, helpless victims whose bodies clutter the battlefield where God and Satan and their armies wage war? *There may be no knowable answers.*

✱ Marshall Fields called about the Oriental rug I ordered. On the way home I stopped in the store and looked at it—

mouthwatering melon pinks and blues and greens. When it was delivered Kris and I lugged it in and spread it out on the floor of the family room. Because it is so beautiful, so centrally effective in enriching the character of the whole house, I long for Harold to see it and love it as much as I do.

✳ Last night I called Jeff and arranged to meet him for dinner to talk about Kris. As I mowed the back lawn for two hours, I thought and prayed for words, and wisdom to say them. As Terry has pointed out, Jeff and I are not a dyad—an equal twosome. I'm a parent with ultimate responsibility for Kris, while he's her brother, who loves her but has no parental authority, nor does he have to bear the consequences for his decisions about her. But I want him to be informed about *why* I'm concerned.

It was the best talk we've ever had—low-key, non-hostile, non-evasive, open and revealing. We were together for two hours and I left him, having gained much more peace of mind. Jeff assured me that he understood how I felt and would support my decisions. But no more of Kris spending the night at his house or driving around Chicago at 4:00 A.M. with his friends!

When I told Kris she couldn't go to the barbecue at Jeff's, she disappeared into her room for several hours. Later I went in to see her, and she was sobbing. I could tell she thought her life wasn't worth living and told her I understood how she felt, was sorry, but that my decision would stand because I felt it was the right one. "But I didn't do anything wrong! So why should I be punished?" "This isn't punishment; it's protection. That's what I have to do until you're mature enough to protect yourself." I left her to think and work it through. I had prayed about it so much, hadn't compromised, and felt obedient to my own Parent.

191

✳ Last week we cleaned out much of Harold's office at 388 Gundersen—reorganized all the bookshelves, purged the files. We plan to use the office as a conference room, and I'm getting one of my color photographs of him enlarged and framed to hang under his antique clock in the corner of the room, against the walnut paneling.

Bit by bit we seem to be erasing the world as Harold saw it, the things he touched and used. It doesn't wipe out the real Harold, nor all he accomplished. But losing these little reminders loosens the ties, makes his person more remote.

✳ Veterans Day. I am filled with longing for my own veteran on a day dark with fine rain and low cloud. But when I drive over to Bronswood Cemetery, I cannot identify Harold's gravesite.

The grassy slope is like a patchwork; under which unmarked square of green does Harold lie? It is a lost kind of feeling, standing in the rain on the ragged grass carved with many more recent burials, not knowing where my husband is. His grave is unmarked because I've had no response yet from the Veterans' Administration, to whom I am applying for a grave marker. So his place is unknown except to God; he's encased in sod that is waking to spring, lying alone unwaking in our double grave as I lie alone in my double bed.

✳ Marian has sent me a photo she took of Harold and me on my last birthday, just a month before his death. He is sitting in his chair in the family room, and I am kneeling in front of him, my arms crossed on his knees, bending toward him, touching his lips with mine. The lamp behind us silhouettes a moment of gentle tenderness.

The picture is a symbol of all the loving, longed-for acts and responses of marriage. Looking at it now gives me great joy and great pain—joy to have a moment captured, the actuality of it, the very way our hands were angled, our heads inclined, the real clothes we wore, the placing of mouth on mouth. Pain because such moments have ceased, and memory is all I have left of love.

I want Harold. But if I can't have him, God, I ask you to fill my odd, human-shaped emptiness.

✱ I've been reading May Sarton's *Mrs. Stevens Hears the Mermaids Singing*—a novel about a poet and her muses which says some remarkable things about the reasons for poetry— that its catalyst is intense personal relationships.

One of her statements rings in me like a gong: "Loneliness is the poverty of self; solitude is the richness of self." For the mystics, solitude was also the richness of the Spirit within and the presence of God. As I think about my own poetry, my heart-cry is that my muse be the mind of Christ within me, that my poetry's catalyst may be an intense, sustained love-making with my Maker who has also promised to be my Husband.

✱ The rain of last week made the grass grow like green fur. Twice Kris and I tried without success to start the mower. The third time, Wednesday night, I prevailed on her to try again. She has a way with machines and knows instinctively, better than I, what to do with them. She stuck with it until she got it going, then remarked, "That was God!"

I am greening too. The winter of bereavement and depression, which for me has lasted at least eighteen months, is over and gone. I am beginning again to stretch up to the sun. There is a fresh growth, beauty instead of ashes. The wounded body of earth is being healed over by the new skin of sod.

VI

A WIND OF CHANGE

June–December 1986

A poet must go unprotected that he may be constantly changed.

—GERALD HEARD, *quoted in May Sarton's* **Journal of a Solitude**

One

Our thirty-third anniversary. I'm alone—one on an anniversary for two, but I feel at peace, buoyed up on love and light, happy that my partner is also at peace, also surrounded by love and light.

Mark and Robin's new house is full of light and space, by comparison with their little rented farm. Her touch is everywhere.

Now I'm sitting on the weathered wooden steps leading up to her front door, flanked by diverse flowerpots packed with the bright colors and fresh green that seem a natural part of the Northwest, with its coolness and rain.

It was pouring when I woke at 6:30. I lay and watched through the window the trickle from the downspout as it thickened to a rope of clear water, then stopped abruptly with the clearing sky. Light suddenly burgeoned to brilliant sun. I dressed quietly, and went out with map and camera. Drove up Sehome Hill into an arboretum of huge conifers dripping and glistening in the horizontal shafts of sun, the mist steaming up from the steep paved road. There was perfect silence but for the birds whose calls echoed along the steep slopes. My camera is a good companion, preserving for me the fresh, woodsy look of ferns and buttercups and old man's beard and wild phlox among the huge trees. Sang aloud and unabashed, "I praise you now, O Lord, with heart and hand and voice."

On Sunday we went to the church that houses four-year-old Lindsay's excellent daycare center. The worship was lovely, warm but not rowdy, but the hour-long sermon, in a warning mode about cults, was full of categorical denunciations of any but the preacher's way of thinking; it rankled us all. Perhaps the tension is between rational certainty and mystery. What may we know for sure, through logic? What must be accepted by faith because we are too limited to understand it? *God, you are going to have to demarcate this for me.*

Over lunch we discussed the sermon. Robin was troubled by its exclusiveness. Funny how in such situations I argue for the conservative (but not fossilized) Christian position. I want for my children the certainties that I cannot always claim for myself. I want them to be safe and sure and loyal. Is this a heart-indicator of where I really am—deep under all the fears and questions? Or is it just where I want to be?

Another part of me says that watertight certainty is like legalism; it jettisons mystery, makes faith unnecessary, grabs the control out of God's hands, and sets up human rules instead. None of us wants that. It's like charting a course in Puget Sound, among all the islands and hidden reefs. We can see the islands and steer clear of obvious obstacles, but the underwater sand and rock bars are mysteries we cannot see, places where we must trust the charts.

On a sunny day, with the tide at a record low, we drove to Chuckanut Bay where the mud-and-sand flats were dotted with clam diggers. The Bay was sheeted with pale green seaweed that stretched moistly for miles—like a woman caught sunbathing in her underwear.

As we picked our way across the bay, we had to avoid

dozens of dead, stranded crabs. Lindsay's comment: "Oh look, Grammy, another baby crab taking a little nap!"

Wind and water have knuckled lovely dimples and scrolls and hollows into the sandstone—dramatic examples of natural sculpture. Some of the rocks rear up like breaking waves, as if they have taken on the character of the forces that molded them. The colors are creamy grays and charcoals under the brick-red of the great madrona tree trunks. I photographed madly.

The drive to Mt. Baker is colored with memories of Harold. Stopping off at Nooksack Falls on the way up, with its roar of icy water between boulders and banks of dark forests, I feel the sharp pang of missing him. We'd stopped together here by the mountain roadside and looked down the valley. And here is where the snow started to fall, and Harold felt dizzy in the thin air. And here we saw a deer—

The sky spattered and shone alternately, but at the top, where the road ends, the scenery was spectacular—ice-blue glaciers and snow and black rocks above the treeline.

In a valley we saw a perfect double rainbow arc-ing across from mountain to mountain, the inner circle spectacularly brilliant, the outer one, its colors reversed, paler, wider, more diffused. I couldn't get the whole shining crescent into my viewfinder. One never can. The camera remembers precisely; but it is also frames, fragments, pulls rectangles out of the air, focuses on the part rather than the whole. Like human experience. Like poetry.

✳ Home to Robin's again. On the telephone answering machine was a message that Grandma Shaw had died, at 98— just a few words from Marion Borg "to let us know what had happened." It hit me suddenly and very hard. I lay face-down on the bed and cried. Besides the tenderness between us, I felt the loss of all that she stood for—her matriarchal quality—the significance she had held for so long to her children and their children, and their children—all the rungs on the generational ladder. And coming so close on the heels of Harold's dying, I felt the aloneness of being pushed, myself, up closer to the pinnacle of age and responsibility and leadership.

✱ A letter from Madeleine tells of Hugh's prostate surgery and the discovery of a malignant bladder tumor. Another cancer arrow strikes. Kris and I are both shaken; Hugh is one of our favorite people.

✱ At the Seattle Pacific dorm where I was housed for a writer's conference, there was a note from Margaret Smith on my door. We'd never met, except in letters. She's one of the few who look just like my internal preview of her—rosy-cheeked, brown-haired, with candid eyes and a serious expression. But when she smiles her whole face bursts into flower. We bonded in an extraordinary way and for the next few days we enjoyed moving in and out of each other's lives and thinking, sharing journals. We find we can talk in a kind of verbal shorthand and our allusions catch and hold and need no explanation. There's no age gap, either, though she's as young as my own daughters. She gave me a lapel button: "So many books; so little time."

After the conference Margaret and I drove south toward Oregon, where she was to meet her husband Jack. I'm coming out to see her later, at their home on the coast, near Astoria.

✱ I'm up early. A small creek runs past the Smith's house in Astoria, water brown as coffee. On the opposite bank flutters a covey of Steller's jays, indigo blue and slighter than standard blue jays. I photographed the creek, and a jeweled spiderweb stretched on the wooden fence by the back door.

Marg and I drive out between dunes onto the sand, wider than any freeway, and speed along the beach, the lines of breakers crashing left, and pale green sea-grass our boundary on the right. As we drive on the unmarked, bone-smooth sand, we see flotillas of small creatures stranded far in from the waves. There are hundreds of them, each about an inch long. Jellyfish? I pick one up. It has no shell, but a translucent crescent of sail arches along its back above an oval, gelatinous "foot." We learn they are "wind-sailers." I feel an affinity for them, their insignificance on this wide, wide beach. At the mercy of the wind.

After an evening of reading poems, talking about God and Harold, crying, looking at slides with M. and Jack, who is a lieutenant in the Coast Guard, I sleep deeply in the loft of their home and wake to find that Margaret, with perfect sensitivity, has left on the night table a book open at a poem by George Herbert:

> And now in age I bud again,
> After so many deaths I live and write;
> I once more smell the dew and rain,
> And relish versing. O my only Light
> It cannot be
> That I am [s]he
> On whom thy tempests fell all night!

✱ Monday morning was sun through the skylight. I gave Marg a pendant, aqua-blue ball of glass melted down and blown from the volcanic ash of Mt. St. Helen. She hung it with its nylon thread in her bathroom.

We drove to Cannon Beach. I'd seen the photos of course—the conical rocks jutting from the water as it spreads its half-mile long crescents of foam along the spread of sand. When there's surf, a mist rises and blurs the distance and the gulls flash in and out of this mystery. My photographs may not work well—the day was too sunny-blue and the photographic drama works better in dark weather. I loved it, wanted to walk more, longer, until I was tired and full of foam and glisten and wind and the far-off roar of the water.

I dreaded saying good-bye. Marg is like John; we have the same eye, see the same things, are moved in similar ways, cry out the same words together at identical moments. We have a contract: I will knit her a sweater and she will weave for me, on her loom, a Luci Shawl.

* Called Madeleine when I got home. Hugh has had severe cis-platinum chemo side effects—"everything in the book," she says. He had only just returned home from the hospital. "Now I'm his nurse," says Madeleine. "But you know all about that."

* I've been dreading this day. In the past, July 4 was always a family picnic and fireworks-at-the-fairgrounds. But you can't exactly "picnic" alone. I called Jeff yesterday and asked if he had plans, and felt an enormous sense of relief when he said, "Well, I was hoping to come out for the weekend."

Jeff and I spent most of this afternoon cutting grass. It's hot and so we got out the ice-cream freezer and developed some great strawberry ice cream. Grilled steaks, and ended up with six of Jeff's friends for the meal. It was a *neat* evening. The guys had a "fireworks fight" in the back yard, while I looked on in horror. But no one lost any vital organs. Then we all played Scrabble and Jeff put a Brahms trio tape on the stereo. I don't know if it was a special "keep Mom from feeling lonely" effort, but it worked!

✱ I bought some Yardley's Old English Lavender soap—a favorite of ours for years. As I used it in the shower today the familiar, spicy smell brought back Harold so strongly that tears rained down my skin with the shower spray.

And while screening trays of slides for possible book jackets, again and again I felt the pleasure/pain of seeing Harold, solid and smiling and untouched by disease—his tan, the hair on the firm flesh of his arms, his old blue corduroys.

In Colson's yesterday I saw an Arrow shirt sale (H.'s favorite brand) and before I could think about it, I was looking through them for his size, 16/33.

Then, while sorting my collected discards for the St. Mark's rummage sale, I found a carton of H.'s old underwear in a pile, just as it had always sat in his bureau drawer—as if I'd washed and folded it for him to wear this week. How can it be true that he'll never use it again? The ordinariness of it—stacked there as if nothing had changed. I buried my face in the soft cloth and wept.

✱ An awful shock today. Joe Bayly died after heart surgery at Mayo Clinic. Dear Joe. He gave so many people the gift of counsel in loss. I remember going to his seminar, "Coping with Grief," last spring. I came into the auditorium late, but when he saw me he stopped, came down from the dais and across the room to hug me. We'll all miss him. The friend who called me said, "He and Harold were a lot alike; people could *rely* on them." Such events intrude in an uncompromising and shocking way.

Death *rarely* fits. It seldom seems right—a tear in the fabric of our own self-determination and independence.

People ask, "Are you over it yet?"

"Am I over it?" Bereavement isn't like measles or the common cold that arrive and disappear without fore- and after-thought. What *is* happening is that I'm accepting the fact of Harold's death at a more profound level. Only rarely now do I stop and tell myself, incredulous, "This must be a nightmare. It can't be real." The certainty of relationship over thirty-three years is beginning to be replaced by the certainty of my being solitary.

And oh, my darling Harold, the world you lived in with me is changing so fast. In just six months you would have trouble recognizing it. There are new stop lights at Gary Ave. and St. Charles Road. New office buildings are raising their square profiles from the weedy fields on the way to work. I wear new clothes you never saw. We're publishing books you had no knowledge of. I am reading manuscripts from new authors. Your children are maturing—moving to new homes, bearing new grandchildren who will never know you. The distance in time and emotion is increasing between us. I sometimes feel I cannot bear this strange and transient world without you, and yet I am, and must be, part of the change.

✱ Margaret put it all in perspective recently. "To live in this world," she quoted in a letter, "you must be able to do three things: to love what is mortal; to hold it against your bones knowing your own life depends on it; and, when the time comes, to let it go, to let it go."

Two

Last Sunday I did a funny thing in church. On impulse, I took the wedding band and our twenty-fifth anniversary ring and diamond off my left hand and tried it on my right. My surface reason was that I wanted to see what it looked like, just as I try on new shoes when I get home from a shopping trip, even though I already know how they look. Unfortunately, the fit of the ring on the ring finger of the right hand is much tighter, and once I'd urged the rings into place over the joint, they gripped; I couldn't get them off again. They're still there, a week later, which means that they've felt strange, nobby, bulky all week, and that has reminded me, forced me to think more deeply about why I moved them.

I think it was because the rings gave me and others the false impression that I was still married, a normal wife and partner—everything comfortable and companionable and settled. And it was a dishonest statement, because I'm solitary, a single anomaly in a married world. I love my rings. H. and I chose and designed them together and I often wear his ring on a chain around my neck. But my rings are symbols of what *was,* memorials, not signs of present reality.

To change rings from hand to hand seems a simple thing. Unsensational. But my left hand refuses to forget, and six days later around the ring finger is a channel of pale, untanned skin where the gold has pressed its shape into me for all my married years. I feel that there's a similar invisible scar of love around my heart. It may be healing, but it will never quite disappear.

✱ Studying on and off all week, I have felt great anxiety about taking the Lay Reader's exam. Wednesday I called Donna Lobs about my panic and she "talked me down," like an air traffic controller. She's so confident that I'll pass. Everyone is. But the amount of detail to be reviewed and absorbed is huge and, even with sample tests to study from, I have to *guess* what will be emphasized.

So I took lots of precautions. Went to Morning Prayer with Rick Thursday and then to his office to ask him questions I couldn't find answers to, and to discuss with him, as the license requires, my "rule of life." He too was heartily reassuring. I studied most of the day and in the evening went to dinner with Joyce and David Fletcher, who had both taken the exam in Spring; asked more questions. They felt I was thoroughly prepared. But the panic persists.

This morning, stuffed to the gills with dates, church councils and codicils, bishops, saints, creeds, biblical trivia, church history, theology, liturgies, I arrived at St. Christopher's in Oak Park. I was the only candidate taking the exam, so Fr. Allen set me up at his own desk and prayed for me as I began. The exam was in two parts and took three hours. The first part, though tricky, I managed well. The priest marked it on the spot and I scored high. The second part, dealing with the use of the lectionary and technical aspects of the Chicago diocese, was harder. I guessed a lot and barely passed. But the relief at passing was great. When I got home and called Donna, and

David Fletcher, they both said, "Well, good. But we knew you'd do fine." Like, "No big deal."

But to me it was a big deal—my first exam in years and years. I wanted someone to celebrate with me. And then, a great surprise: As I used up the last sheet of paper on an old memo pad of Harold's, I came across some words in his writing on the cardboard backing (evidently a rough draft of his message of congratulation to John when he got his M.D.). I took the words as his special message to me after my test: "Hooray! You've passed another milestone! Congratulations, and all my love and appreciation."

I realize my need these days for a single, solid, central human relationship. I have trouble maintaining perspective on my own. I have so many *good* friends, and some *great, close* friends, and I can call on my kids any time, but a ten-minute phone call, or even a meal or an evening together, is no substitute for the consistency and integration of marriage.

✳ Psalm 66, the lectionary psalm for today, says:

> Bless our God ... who holds our souls in life
> and will not allow our feet to slip.
> For you, O God, have proved us;
> you have tried us just as silver is tried.
> You brought us into a snare;
> you laid heavy burdens on our backs.
> You let enemies ride over our heads.
> We went through fire and water,
> But you brought us out into a place of
>   refreshment.

I like the "we" and "our" of that. May all of it prove true for me, for my children, for countless others who struggle.

✳ Monday morning John called from Japan, his Navy transfer orders having come through; his "window" (the possible arrival date) opens sometime in the first two weeks of September. My plan is to meet him in San Francisco and drive with him in the new Honda he is bringing back from Japan, to Bellingham, then home to Chicago. This will give us some needed time together before his residency in Pensacola. I look forward to that event so strongly I'm scared.

Later in the month, though, is the birth of Marian's baby, delivery date unknown. She wants me to be with her during labor. Can these unplannable things fit together smoothly?

✳ Today would have been Harold's birthday. *My dearest, I have no gifts for you but flowers on the altar in church, in memory of you, and my love and appreciation for all you were and still are in my imagination. Though this is your seventieth birthday you'll never be seventy. How good that I'll be able to think of you always as you were in your prime, before cancer—glowing with life, youthful for your age, steadfast, warm, ardent in spirit and in body.*

I'm missing him dreadfully. It comes in waves or gusts like the storm the other afternoon, when the wind actually became visible in the bursts of rain swept along in it. But such storms are normal for us in August. I listen to what C. S. Lewis said in *A Grief Observed:* "Bereavement is an integral part of our experience of love. It follows marriage as normally as marriage follows courtship, or as autumn follows summer. It is not a truncation of the process but one of its phases; not the interruption of the dance but its next figure."

The ache of the unattainable, the transient. Heading home with Kris, the horizon bisected the sun so that its blinding sphere dazzled our eyes over the fields. Behind us the clouds were purple, riffled and conflated along the eastern horizon like an aerial mountain range bathed in pink—outlines sharp and clear in the cool, crystal air. They looked so close, not forty miles away. The westward clouds were stratified, lined and edged with gold from the sun, not brassy, but tender as they melted and dimmed.

Now we're home. Now I have the camera. But it's too late. I cannot film what has faded and disappeared. The impression, the loveliness of it, stays in my mind, but without the force of the original. And new cloud formations will never duplicate the old. As the future will never duplicate the past.

* John will arrive in San Francisco on September 5! I have made plans to join him on the 6th. Moments after I had booked my flight, Carol Raffensperger called me from work. "Are you free? Can you go sailing with me September 1–5?" Glory on glory—the dates work! No conflicts, and I can even be present for the Lay Readers' commissioning on August 31. The whole plan seems to fit so cleanly, like the last pieces slipped into a jigsaw puzzle. I have been praying about this. I should easily make it back home in time to do the grandmothering bit for Marian in Indianapolis.

Three

I'm in another world. Carol R. and I are snugly ensconced in a 28-foot sailboat in the Anchor Marine harbor at Sister Bay, Wisconsin. Gentle waves lap at our boat's underside, and the air is cool and quiet. Through the porthole I can see a star.

The owner was skeptical when we chartered the boat. He is accustomed to dealing with men or couples. Grim-faced, he pointed out the battered hull of a sailboat that had been hauled off the rocks a few miles north days before because the skipper had taken chances. The lives of four people were in jeopardy during the rescue.

But Carol has owned and sailed boats most of her adult life, and her obvious knowledge and expertise must have reassured him. For two single women, one on the edge of a divorce, one a new widow, this is adventure. It is also risk, as is most adventure. Carol and I are each beginning a new voyage.

We're glad we planned ahead—woolen clothes in layers, slickers, deck shoes, nourishing, easy-to-prepare food, sleeping bags, cameras, journals, and a mini-library of books to read in harbor at night. Our check-out man, with the reassuring name of Lincoln, took us through "Acquittal" item by item—the generator, the dinghy, the propane stove, the two-way radio, what jibs to use when, and a long list of how-tos: how to pump out the head, how to start the diesel engine, how to avoid blowing all the fuses, how to call Anchor Marine for help, how to raise the Coast Guard, how to read the depth-sounder and odometer and compass and most important of all, how to read the charts.

The level of Green Bay, in fact, all of Lake Michigan, is five feet higher than two years ago. The charts have to be read keeping in mind that some reefs and small islands are submerged. It's a metaphor of faith. You believe and go by the chart rather than by what eyes and binoculars see.

Today the water is flat calm, smooth as obsidian. When the wind ruffles its surface it looks like a seamless yardage of gray silk, with the gulls floating on it like slubs in the fabric. We pass bluff after bluff, each looking like the end of the world until we round it and see the next. The most fearsome point of all, Death's Door, site of many shipwrecks, looks deceptively mild and protective in the oily calm.

After a gentle crossing of open water, we reach Washington Island and follow the line of red buoys round the channel into the perfect little crescent-shaped harbor with a low, fringed, reedy spit of land sheltering our anchorage. By now the sun has burned the fog away, blue crowds out gray, and suddenly it's hot. We anchor. Swimsuited, we dive into the icy green water and swim while shampooing our hair, then lie deliciously on the deck and sun like cats. There is no intrusive noise—no breakers crashing, no motors running—just enough moving air to keep us from sweltering. A remote buoy horn sounds regularly, like a small, systematic ghost.

✱ Tonight the air is chill and we are sunburned and the sleeping bags feel good. The compactness of a boat demands

211

orderliness; everything has to have its place. But it feels so cozy. To save the engine batteries we're both reading and writing by candlelight. The quietness hums, it crowds the ears; one can almost hear the atoms pinging. The couple of candles shed a meager radiance. The boat moves ever so slightly as though touched by a child's single finger.

* Running before the wind can be a lovely, easy, rhythmic business, but this is forceful enough to be a little scary, particularly after leaving Washington Island, Rock Island, St. Martin's Island behind. We are out of sight of any land. The horizon is blurred by fog or rain; we think, though we can't be sure, that we are on the correct heading for Fayette.

* It's hard to concentrate tonight—a front has passed through and the clouds are scudding by like rags, revealing or obscuring stars. At anchor in Snail Shell Harbor, there is a constant humming—the vibration of the wind through the stays—and flashes of sheet lightning (like God showing himself in the dark).

* I don't know the date and I don't care. We woke to a clearish day, but with pink clouds to the East—a warning. Raised anchor at 6:30 and motored out of the harbor and into a strong SE wind.

The air is darker, full of low clouds and mist, and the wind has freshened even more. We heard from a couple of other sailors that this morning's forecast of a change of wind from SE to NE has been revised and the south winds are to continue,

212

with rain, all day tomorrow. We have visions of the long return trip to Sister Bay, using the motor or beating into the wind—an unappealing prospect. I'm anxious. Will we make it back in time to get to Chicago for my flight? For the first time, I am forced out of the present into a concern that lies beyond this wild remoteness.

✴ We must have bucked a hundred thousand waves, and every one spat in our faces, drenching us. In the spray they lifted into the air beaded starbursts of watered light in which we saw rainbows, single, double, close enough so that we could reach out and put our hands through them.

Coming in sight of Anchor Marine at last, jammed with boats sheltering from the wild weather, we see Lincoln waving us to a mooring outside the breakwater. I drop and wrap the main and ready bow and stern springlines and bumpers. Carol brings us in, heading into the wind—a letter-perfect docking, while Lincoln shouts, "I'd take you two on as crew any day. Couldn't have done it better myself!" We feel triumphant.

Two women—single, though not by choice—facing lives that can be as sunny and calm, or as stormy and fierce as Lake Michigan. We are learning to sail our ships. There are some charts, a compass, a depth sounder, and a wind that lifts and languishes by turns. But it is never a boring voyage.

Four

How extraordinary, and yet how natural and ordinary it seems to be with John again! After picking up my bag we went to San Francisco's International Terminal and the USO to check for his missing suitcase, which could have been waylaid in any one of four airports en route from Iwakuni.

Yesterday was a tale of phone calls. John's car "should be" available for him Thursday, possibly Wednesday. And his suitcase turned up in Clark Air Force Base in the Philippines and "should be" delivered at the airport here Friday.

* I've been reading Earl Wilson's *The Undivided Self* and find this statement such a true reflection of my recent experience of God at work to order my circumstances: "When we take time to trust God, we find that the thankful feelings which are thus generated encourage us to trust him the next time we have something to do. In fact, when our attitude is positive, we find new faith to energize our Christian lives. Faith while doing holds our various activities together so they begin to make sense." I'm beginning to see the truth of this worked out in life—seeing the disjunctive pieces of plans come together gives me confidence (faith) that as I look to God for help, and choose to expect it, he will do the same for me again.

✻ How neatly everything has worked out! Yesterday John called the car forwarding agency and was told that the Honda had cleared customs and insurance at the docks and would be at the agent's office within the hour.

The car sat in a row of others, looking smug and sleek under its satiny red skin. We transferred our baggage, filled up with gas, and took off into the heavy traffic to the Oakland Bay Bridge and the airport, where John ran in and claimed his suitcase. I could see the relief on his face to finally have his belongings. (How hard we hold on to these extensions of our physical bodies. What is the spiritual counterpart?)

Madeleine and Hugh were in my mind a lot yesterday—the day of his surgery for removal of a cancerous bladder. I turned my thoughts into arrows of prayer.

✻ John and I drove to Bellingham through the long, flat stretch of the Napa Valley with its sere mountains to the west, hung with sun in shades of gold, purple, rose.

As we drove further north, the higher elevations of Oregon and Washington were still and silent, the air fresh from showers scented with balsam, the short thick ground cover tinted wine and copper and sparkling with clear drops, and the dull purple of wild blueberries. Dwarfs of spruce and pine have clamped themselves into the gray, stratified rocks, handsome as bonsai, formations of strong, fluid, natural design.

Delight fills the air, the exhilarating power and purity of

height and view. Every angle reveals itself as uniquely beautiful—the jutting peaks, the deep indigoes of distance, the contrasts of dark and light on the clouds, with uncorrupted blue between them. The boom of a sudden avalanche astounds us, its large sound ricocheting around a valley.

For some time I've been wanting a cabin for vacation and writing. It would be fun to design a small home and build it here, with Mark as the contractor.

Thursday morning we looked at lots in Sudden Valley. Of three possibilities, I liked best the one bordered on two sides by a clear creek, well-wooded, with a clearing in the center and an enormous Sitka spruce dominating the space. Three deer were feeding among the alder saplings, so unafraid they ignored us as we walked within a couple of feet of them. It seemed like a welcome.

✻ An early morning roadscape furred with fog—needle-points of pines pushing up to the light. The sun is a pearl that appears, dim, in its sea of mist, displays its milky iridescence, then withdraws. John and I are leaving Bellingham after five days. I click a photo every now and then through the window as we speed south to Sedro Woolley where we'll turn east through the Cascades.

✻ We've tented for two nights now, using our little canvas pup tent with a broomstick for a tent pole! We got a little hysterical in the night when the stake holding the tent pole fell down and we were swathed in damp folds of rubbery canvas in the dark!

Five hundred miles of Idaho, Montana, and Wyoming lay between our first and next campsites—miles of rain, brilliant clouds, and clouds lead-heavy with sleet and snow. Raced through steep valleys and snow showers toward Yellowstone in gathering darkness and set up our tent at a camp near the Western Entrance while there was still a little light. We were the only tenters. "Going to tough it out, are you?" asked the park ranger, with a wry look. "Have you heard the forecast?" "No. What is it?" "Hard freeze, and snow by morning."

We put on all our warm sweatshirts and crawled into our bags high on the Continental Divide. The thin foam pads didn't erase the stones of the ground beneath us. But only my nose was cold, poking out of my sweatshirt hood.

As we peeked out through the tent flaps early this morning, the grass glistened with diamonds of snow in the rising sunlight. Driving through Yellowstone, we saw a million pines like Christmas trees tufted with snow. The lakes and rivers steamed in the frigid air, and thermal pools boiled fiercely—a mephistophelian landscape.

✱ Driving east. John and I have been talking about Psalm 37 which I'd been reading earlier. Again and again the "righteous" are contrasted with the "wicked." The righteous person is seen to struggle and even despair, but find ultimate reward from God. The wicked prosper temporarily, but end up in hell. John said, "It sure makes you want to be certain you're one of the righteous." Talked about what *righteous* means—not perfect, but with a heart that longs for God as I longed for him in the dark and cold last night, lonely for him, lonely to hear his voice. This psalm in John's *New English Bible* fills me with the ache to be what God wants me to be.

✱ We're traveling the flat lands on a highway almost as straight as an arrow. I feel emotionally flat too, as the climb and plunge of the landscape has been reduced to a series of prairie cornfields relieved by an occasional clump of trees around a farmhouse and silo, or the slump of a gully at the side of the road.

But I'm getting the feel of the new contours. It takes a while to recognize characteristic features, and then look for more of the same, like growing accustomed to a new fashion. Now I'm seeing rolling waves of dun-colored hills with skin like the velvet on a deer's antlers. And shaven wheat fields painted yellow in late afternoon, light against slate-gray storm clouds.

✱ Returned home to receive a call from Madeleine. "Luci, Hugh died this morning." Shock. But why? What were we really expecting? We cried together on the phone, sisters in grief.

✱ Marian has had contractions on and off for days. The question in the air is, can she deliver naturally after having two C-sections? Her doctor specializes in cases like hers. Still laboring fruitlessly she called when I got home and asked me to drive down after supper. I was ready, so I did. Three and a half hours to their Indianapolis door.

The great triumph is that after two C-sections the delivery was natural, without epidural anesthesia, and the baby was healthy. Once she was cleaned up and her squashed little head began to round out, Michelle was beautiful. Marian was euphoric. I called all the people who needed to know.

Karl and I both held the baby and cuddled her, then I drove home to be with the girls. On Wednesday I took them in to see their new sister. She was dressed in pink with a tiny hairbow, her black hair soft and fluffy and her face a perfect pink—a lovely seashell of a baby. They are calling her Shell.

✳ Now that Marian is home I feel more relaxed, dashing around and running errands for her and the kids, with Marian calling the shots. What a joy to see her in her maturity, her fruitfulness, her kind, strong mothering. In this new experience of birthing she has faced herself as she is—still fallible, sometimes disappointed in herself, yet knowing herself capable now of prolonged patience during pain—a twenty-four hour labor progressing to the "push and splash of birth." Like all births, it is an event both natural and miraculous.

Harold knew of Marian's pregnancy before he died. New life was beginning like a small flame kindled, as his was dying out.

Marian and Karl say they miss his prayers for their children. I miss what he stood for. His person integrated around the Christ at his core gave our whole family a stability, a foundation. I can't take his place as a father, but I want to be what God is calling me to be—a mother, a friend, an encourager, one who sets an example of listening to my heavenly Parent.

✳ In reviewing the last six weeks I see now I didn't need to worry about planning around unknowns. Everything took its place in sequence—the sailing trip, the wait in California, our time with the Schramers, a chance to look at real estate in Bellingham, the fun of traveling and tenting our way across the west, my week catching up at the office, Marian going into labor *after* I'd read Scripture at St. Mark's on Sunday, and after the HSP and LBI board meetings, my being with her in her successful labor and delivery—all divinely orchestrated.

Five

Some things suddenly came together in my mind last night. Harold made the quantum leap from Bethany, where public ministry by a woman is forbidden, so I'd have a chance to participate actively in the church's ministry. And now I'm doing it! This Sunday I will read Scripture, lead in the Intercessory Prayer, and bear the chalice during Communion. And now the Bible study is starting, and I'll also be teaching the adult Sunday school in January. Plus, the possibility of full-time writing next Fall at Friends University in Wichita exhilarates me. How happy Harold would be that his hope for me is being realized! I think I am reaching a point where I no longer need or expect all the love and care to come in my direction; I want to start giving it to others; to be free to both receive and give.

I was confident and serene today during the reading of Scripture and Intercessory Prayers. But it was bearing the chalice that gave me the most joy. I felt the intensity and unity of the communion of saints in a new way, the wonder of sharing something of Christ himself—a servant dispensing the Servant—as the words "The blood of our Lord Jesus Christ keep you in everlasting life" were repeated over and over, with personal intent for each communicant at the altar rail. Up until then, the mechanics of the whole thing had distracted me—the "where to stand," the "what to do when" had scattered my focus. Now there is an alertness, an awareness of each individual and the link I am providing between that person and God, no matter how familiar the ritual becomes.

My heart did a leap when I saw Kris kneeling there.

✱ I used to think of myself as a strong person—tough-minded and strong-willed, at any rate. Yet I still have trouble, as I make my bed in the morning, as I smooth the sheets and plump the pillow on Harold's side, preparing a place for the husband who doesn't come to my bed any more. Sometimes I think that rather than making up a double bed where we can lie together and be one, I am digging a grave—that when I go to sleep, I am joining him in the unconsciousness of death. Only, for me, it is temporary. Like Lazarus, I wake to die all over again.

Ironically, when Karen and I had coffee together after the healing Eucharist, she said, "When someone asks me how you're doing, I tell them you're working through bereavement still, but you're doing it as well as anyone I've known."

✱ I walked this morning, for the first time in weeks. No travel schedule, no bad weather to keep me in. A cool, moistly sunny day when Fall showed herself in the descent of leaves— floating straight down in the calm air, or a rustling gust of them in long, angled trajectories when the breeze picked up. Whole banks and yards carpeted, the floors of the woods solid with red and gold.

Hear him, ye deaf,
His praise. ye dumb,
Your loosened tongues employ!

The trees listen to him. He speaks in seasons, and they obey. But we humans, with minds and wills, are less prone to listen because we cannot be still. When Jesus asked for ears to hear, he must have longed for receptacles into which his voice would penetrate and resonate, where his own mind could take root and become part of us. He created, he cares, so he communicates.

Lord, am I allowing this process to happen in me? Yes. All this morning's meditation is the result of your Spirit interacting with mine to show me, on all levels, who you are, how urgent and ardent is your love.

✱ I called Clyde Kilby today in response to his note about my *Wheaton Alumni* article. How much his encouragement has always meant to me—"You're a real poet!" he'd say, and I knew he meant it. Martha came on the phone first, then she called Clyde in from the garden. He sounded winded but cheerful, confessed to restlessness at night from asthma. We talked about the blessings of the Episcopal church. He invited me to "come and visit any time" and concluded, as always, "I love you very much."

I was out of the house all next day getting a freezerload of bread from the day-old bakery store, sealing the bald spots on the driveway, mowing all the grass. I came in at 4:30. Martha Mead was on the phone. She made some comments about what to do about the Kilbys. I didn't catch her drift. She said, aghast, "You mean you haven't heard the news? Dr. Kilby died in his sleep early this morning." I was stunned. He had been so central to me for so long—I had known him longer than I had known Harold. I'm convinced I'm in literature and writing today because of him. How glad I am I called, and heard his voice and felt his warmth. And to die in your sleep—how marvelous! After all those restless nights, to be restless no longer. To finally approach the Truth and the Life you've been talking about, and seeking, all your days.

✱ Kris had a cold and didn't go to church. Driving there alone sometimes seems a lonely business, and this ache of aloneness persisted all day in spite of all the loving looks and talks with people at church. Sometimes being alone is freedom; sometimes it is like a kind of cage which keeps me from stepping far into their lives, and prevents them from entering mine.

I keep calling my kids, with a heart full of love that never quite gets expressed fully or poured out to the bottom. It's never enough—time is short, distances are far, phone calls, letters, visits have beginnings and ends.

In the evening I made a series of phone calls to try to regain a sense of community, of being surrounded by loving ones. Called, among others, Paula D'Arcy in Connecticut. Paula told me that during All Saint's Day Communion that morning she had "seen" her church balcony full of heaven's saints and Harold with them, "shining with light and joy." It was both comforting and wrenching to hear this from her. Why can't I have a vision of him?

The sense of aching loss persisted all next day—the need to hug, to pour out, to release my capped gusher of love. I cried in my room alone, something I can rarely do. Sobbed. Wailed. I was suddenly capable of self-diagnosis. This is what people mean by *heart ache.*

Paradoxically, I'm also hungry to receive love. Is satisfaction possible? Or is love like an appetite that can be temporarily filled but needs to be replenished? There's contentment and fullness after a good meal, a good orgasm, a hot drink on a cold day, and after love and caring expressed and received. But it's never permanent.

Another question: Does love have to wear skin, or can I transfer this emotional need to a spiritual context and be loved by God enough to quench this thirst? I don't think so. If God were enough, why would he have created Eve for Adam?

Karen thinks my deep ache on the weekend *was* my awareness of Harold, of my loss, and that Paula's message was from the Lord to assure me that he's not lost—that he's there, and real.

✱ Met Jeff in Oak Park for dinner last night. We had two hours together of outpoured emotion, of hunger crying out for nourishment. Our eyes can meet each other and weep and hold through the tears, as our hands touch. It was warm relief, like a sodden field steaming in the sun after days of rain. But it was not enough. It was agony to leave him.

On my walk this morning, stalking through early mist with camera, I reflected on my changing emotional weather—the grayness and ache of the weekend was a true reflection of my state. I am bereaved. I have lost. I am alone. Half an hour later, by the end of my walk, the sun was pushing through the frost-fog, warming twigs on the bare trees until they glistened with wetness; crystal drops hung from every woody nub and knob, and the cobwebs, finer than hair, beaded through the air from twig to twig.

Now the sky overhead shines its faint blues through the mist. Light and warmth increase with every second, like the exhilaration I begin now to feel, as part of the landscape. And that, also, is the truth about me.

S̊ix

.... ———————————————————————————————— ....

As I read again the copy Joe McClatchey gave me of his
Wade Lecture on Logres and Arthur and the Matter of Britain
and the Centrality of the Grail, I was caught up in such a logic
of praise I almost levitated. I felt drunk with the Holy Spirit
(which is what Paul told us to be). Under the influence I wrote,
as if to some inner dictation:

Song from the throat

The silver syllable of the new moon speaks the sky.
The trumpet of noon sun articulates zeniths, both past
and to come. Praise! for the plush fields, but also for
wry rocks and the dry, dying brass of deserts. *Gloria,*
  Domine,
for minds ignited with images, for the flames that leap
  from
his tongue to scorch our pages with his true words.
  Exultate!

All sensate beings—Sing, from the throat! With the
  sting

of stigmata, of holy wounds, sharpening the sound,
  weaving
the weft of pleasurable air with the colored warp of
  pain.
Sing! For he comes, his nimbus a rainbow, fair as sun,
  clear
as moon, terrible as an army with banners glittering.
  Jubilate!

Like lightning he fires the fine hairs on our heads
till they gleam and flare—gold threads, silver. He
  polishes
the balls and sockets of our bones unto leaping and
  shivering.
Our loins burn. Our mouths are bells. Our hearts pulse
with holy desire, are transfixed by an invading grace,
  rise
to run, spirited, wearing the weight of glory given.
  Laudate!

In Charles Williams' words, "There was no capable song for
the joy in me."

✱ Leading the Bible study tonight at our house, I felt relaxed
and sensed that the others did too. I recognized insights coming
as I led, and some of the old unused skills in group dynamics
returned. The subject was servanthood. We sang a Scripture
song, "Put on the apron of humility." I wished Harold were
with me. He would have been so happy about starting up a
study again. With people, in Bible study, he shone like the sun.

I am learning to let myself grieve and miss H. and feel the
ache more freely, sinking down into it, not trying to "snap out
of it," not cutting off the flow of memories because they hurt.
He's nearly always in the back of my thinking. I often imagine

what his reactions would be to my daily cries and crises. Perhaps that's why I am feeling his reality a bit more.

In church, during the Prayers of the People, we prayed, "Give to the departed eternal rest. Let light perpetual shine upon them. We praise you for your saints who have entered into joy. May we also come to share in your heavenly kingdom." And I felt *it was so*—that Harold was moving in light, that he knew only joy.

✳ Kris and I were looking at slides taken last Christmas, and suddenly there on the wall was Harold's face, larger than life, features thin and vulnerable, but smiling with a touching, almost childlike eagerness. I just wanted to look and look and look. I couldn't help it—I actually reached out to touch him, but all I felt was the cold, chalky paint of the wall under my fingers. He'd gone flat, one-dimensional, as though he were a trick of light.

I had one of the worst nights since Harold's death. Slept scarcely at all—lay in the dark gnawed by fear and anxiety and loneliness. No one, specific worry—just an overwhelming of spirit. Maybe it's a result of shorter daylight, longer nights, the cold and snow, the looming holidays complete with a score of reminders that this year will be, is, different. I dread Christmas shopping and the sending of hundreds of cards. The baking and the present-giving hold no joy for me. I know things will get both better and worse as time goes on.

I went to see Terry for the first time in two months. Her manner toward me seems different; she listens with interest and respect. I told her of some recent attacks of anxiety, and she warned me against using alcohol or tranquilizers to ease pain. Evidently the female metabolism of such substances makes them more dangerous. And anyway, as Emily Dickinson says: "Narcotics cannot still the tooth that nibbles in the soul."

She asked if I were afraid of death. No. Of failing. In one way, dying would be a welcome release from this trap of responsibility and my fear of failure.

The fear of being alone while I was in Florida is a picture of the panic of my whole life—of not being good enough, or strong enough, or capable enough to deal with personal crisis. Rather than facing the problem fully and wading through it, I run for the nearest help—taking a pill, calling family or friends, anything to dull the pain and make me feel better.

But the good feeling is temporary. It fades. I realize that if I could break through to life without the fear of failing, it would be like being born all over again!

Terry suggested another analogy—of a heart defect. Rather than undergo radical surgery, with all its inherent risk, I have chosen for years to live with the problem, adapting my life style to the restricted existence of a "heart" patient. My life has not been without value, but the flaw, the defect, still lodges in the heart. I need to submit to the Surgeon and go through open-heart surgery and come out mended and whole for the first time in my life. How? I have to puzzle that out with myself and God. I must wait for the heartache to come again, and not try to kill the pain by myself.

Terry thinks, though, that those months of therapy have built up my consciousness of God, and of myself as a real person, to the point where he and I *can* walk through the panic together. It's the Job experience, waiting on the ash heap, listening for God's answer.

For a very long time God didn't respond to Job. If I keep calling on other people to rescue me from the silence of God, God himself will remain silent and leave me stranded on the Ash Heap. I must listen for him, be rescued by him. Only.

My current agreement with Terry and God: to trust him rather than running for help, or distracting myself from anxiety. If I call Terry she will not rescue me. She has agreed, rather, to trust God along with me.

✱ Back in Bellingham and Sudden Valley. I am assailed by steep waves of anxiety. Am I planning wisely for the future? Will building a new home inhibit my giving? Will the monthly payments strangle me? Mark tried to reassure me; together we prayed about it, and when Robin and Kris returned from a tour of Western Washington University, we all went out to see the lot.

The sky was clear enough overhead on the drive out to see Mt. Baker's white cap sharply outlined above the foothills, mist drifting in at the lower level. The lot was staked out by the surveyors yesterday. They hacked a sort of low tunnel through the densely massed balsams along the back lot line so we can walk through behind the giant Sitka spruce to the far corner, which is on the opposite side of the stream, staked red in the gravelly sand bank.

The land is so thickly overgrown with brush and saplings it is impossible to see all four corners of the lot at once. One must survey with the eyes of faith. But looking up through the trees, to the south, the sky is a glowing blue, patterned with pink clouds lit with sun from below the line of mountains. The smell of cedars and humus fills the air. The bushes are hung with drops, each holding its glint of light, and the damp leaf mold underfoot is dotted with moonplants, moss, bracken, and little flowerlike white mushrooms with ragged "petals." The stream seems fuller and faster than last Fall when John and I had stood on the pebbly island in its middle. It curves around the edges of the ponderous, mossy boulders that support the soil well above water level. I respond to this setting emotionally, embracing it, enjoying it, wanting to settle in, to feel its permanence.

I am caught between excitement and nervousness about this venture. In the night I lay awake and trembled helplessly about it all. It suddenly occurred to me that this is an anxiety to be lived through and not rescued from, an opportunity to place myself in God's hands. After all, I have prayed about building here, and I have to believe God is directing me, has placed within me this strong pull to the Pacific Northwest.

I do love the thought of an interesting, esthetically satisfying home in that wonderful green setting. I love the creative juices that are beginning to flow to make it happen. I feel a strong urge to get on with it. Yet nausea and cramps combine to drain me of energy. Is it related to my uncertainty about the house?

Now our visit is over and we are on the highway again, moving south to Seattle and the airport, Kris is driving (I feel too tired to drive). Turned on a Christian radio station (the kind I usually shun). The program began with a benediction. What a surprising sense of comfort and meaning it imparted, like a message beamed directly to me.

Then the words of a song: "Though I feel uneasy, I know his way is best, and he'll be with me." My eyes fill with tears. I affirm the truth that God is with me; it resonates with my own need for reassurance. Kris tells me she "feels good" about Western Washington U. That too brightens the picture and confirms the direction.

✳ Today, for the first time in ages, I had guests for dinner—the Mains and the Bosches. I feel unaccustomed to festive cooking, and the ideas for varied meals no longer flow easily to mind. Having a hungry and appreciative husband to cook for was supreme culinary motivation. David prayed before the meal, thanking God for all the memories of meals in our dining room with Harold at the head of the table. Now, without him, it's never quite full, no matter how many guests we have.

✳ Monday was the feast of St. Thomas, and Rick made the telling point that while some people are skeptical, asking questions to disprove God, Thomas's questions burst out of him because he wanted so badly to *believe*. My experience exactly. Rick thinks Thomas was a distinct personality type; for him, belief had to be grounded on the deepest reality, not mere superficial acceptance or supposition.

I visited with Rick afterwards and thought through with him the pros and cons of my serving on the vestry. We both came to the clear conclusion that this is not the time for me to take on such a responsibility. My call is to write. As I have already told Steve at HSP, I am clearing my schedule of editing and speaking to allow more time for writing. It would be counterproductive for me to fill that space with more committee work, necessary though it is for the parish.

✱ The Christmas cards are arriving in great piles. I sat at the cluttered breakfast room table and opened and opened them, the tears falling on the writing of my friends. Again and again they assure me, "Our prayers and love are with you this Christmas."

A card from Sue and Jim Nicodem with recollections of Harold. He stood "one Sunday morning at Bethany Chapel (in 1976) and spontaneously read aloud: 'I was young and now I am old, yet I have *never* seen the righteous forsaken, or their children begging bread.' And then he sat down. His name is written in my Bible by that verse," Sue explained, "and the truth of it was written on my heart because of your examples of faith and love." Dear Sue. Those words struck me, plangent as the clang of bells. And it's true—God has not forsaken us nor made us beggars.

The Boards sent a card that made me cry—"I know this has been a difficult year for you, surely one of the hardest of your life. But it has not been hard for me. It's been a great year despite the strain of a new company and a new role, and you have made it a great year for me. Thanks for your gentle and godly leadership. For 1987 we are bold to pray that God will turn your mourning into dancing in his own way and time. I'm encouraged to see you live in the present and the future, rather than in the past—Much love, Steve and Nancy."

✱ All Christmas Day I managed to fend off emotion—kept it at arm's length with determined cheerfulness, not just for my own sake but for the kids'. The only somber moment was when Jeff, alone with me momentarily, told me his depression and despair on finding out that Vickie is going out with another man. "We both knew the relationship couldn't work," he said, "but when she told me she was seeing someone else, it was awful. I feel so alone." All I could do was hold his hand and cry and tell him I understood and I pray every day for the right woman for him. "Yes."

In the mail came a book from Word—*The Myth of Certainty* by Daniel Taylor—which addresses "reflective" Christians and their questions and in which I recognize myself on every page. And a cut crystal, round, the size of a walnut, from Elizabeth Rooney. I've strung it up in the dining room window. Even on a gray day it sparkles, holding within itself changing angles of color for me to enjoy.

Saturday, more treasures. Margaret's Luci Shawl—handwoven and thickly subtle, with a warmth all its own because it came from her. And the drawn-to-scale plans of the house from Mark. I'm studying them, pleased with his thoroughness and careful planning.

✱ Kris is so companionable today. We chatted like friends—making ordinary, nonsignificant small talk. Except that it is significant to me because it signals a change, an easing, an acceptance. She and Jeff took me to the Hamlet for my birthday dinner. How I love my kids—they're close and warm on a cold night. I thank God for them.

* My birthday, and a party for me at the Mains'. Carol Raff. is invited too, and we drive over together. Angels are everywhere in Karen's house, especially at Christmas. The house glows with white candles. The whole Group is together for the first time since Spring. The predetermined topic of conversation: "What Do I Want to Be Like When I Am Old?" David wants to be like Norman Vincent Peale. Karen wants to be a cross between a solitary contemplative and a pushy, brassy extrovert (quite a trick). Pennie wants to be "Totally taken up with good works." Donna and Rick, if either outlives the other, want to become monastics. Jack wants to be a lover of children and old people. Carolyn and I want to sail around the world. Actually, she would like to be a "facilitator and lover," and I wish never to run out of questions to ask, and to grow broader rather than narrower in my outlook.

While we were eating Karen's "deep, dark secret" dessert, the doorbell rang and a classical guitarist arrived with wife and guitar, to give us a private concert! It was a birthday to link with last year's—same group, same loving, creative thoughtfulness—yet so different without Harold.

* I feel a sharp course redirection for the coming year. The wind is changing. I am reminded of a time last summer when Carol Raff. and I, on our sailing trip together, were planning how to bring our craft back to home port in heavy weather.

Lying in my sleeping bag in Snail Shell Harbor that night

with the rain pelting down and no assurance about the morning's weather or our return to Sister Bay on schedule, I deliberately handed over anxiety to God and claimed and received heart peace. I can remember the actual moment. I was looking up at the small rectangular porthole, its glass all blistered with raindrops faintly lit, and knew that I didn't have to be in control, that I could trust in God to care for us and blaze a track against the wind, across those monster waves, all the way back to safe harbor. It was a moment of choice, and growth because of choice.

VII

A SECRET STAIR

January–July 1987

. . . Mirth, the holy laughter of a God who seizes everything wrong and assures that it all turns out right . . . there all the time, but never heard unless it's attended to. I hadn't been silent enough. I hadn't learned to wait. *It was the sound of my name in God's mouth, the word that I was created and chosen to be, the part that I have been given in the chorus to shape into song.*

—HAROLD FICKETT, **The Holy Fool**

One

The New Year is in. The old one passed away quietly during the hours of dark and sleep.

John's Pensacola apartment pleases me at every turn. (Kris and I flew in last night.) The off-white walls showcase his Japanese etchings, his posters and photographs, driftwood, and calligraphy. The room is full of artful touches—his personally designed bookcases, a lamp of Japanese driftwood and rice paper, a guitar rack that makes the three guitars on the wall a part of the decor. The rust tablecloth I sent him for Christmas is a perfect complement. Out across the porch one can see maple and pine saplings beyond a sandy stream, their turning colors a living mural.

The sun is shining so seductively here today that I spread a sleeping bag on John's narrow balcony and, in spite of the wintry forty-five degrees, I put on my swimsuit and luxuriated like a cat in a sheltered spot. My skin welcomes the naked heat of the sun. For two contented hours I have lain here, knitting, reading, dozing, meditating on a poem by George MacDonald.

> O Son of man, to right my lot
> Naught but thy presence can avail;

Yet on the road thy wheels are not,
Nor on the sea, thy sail.

My fancied ways, why should'st thou heed?
Thou com'st down thine own secret stair—
Com'st down to answer all my need,
Yea, every bygone prayer.

Again, as so often before, I feel the secret thoughts rising in me, trusting them to be God-thoughts making themselves known. Which started me reflecting on the Spirit, and how he teaches us all things and guides us into truth, as Jesus promised. I checked 1 Corinthians 2:10–16 in John's New International Version of the Bible—about how God reveals things to us. My spirit knows my thoughts; God's Spirit knows God's thoughts. Because I am God's daughter, a bridge, a path, a secret stair has been built from his heart to mine so that by the Spirit God's thoughts can step into my mind. "This is what we speak, not in words taught us by human wisdom, but in words taught by the Spirit. . . . The spiritual person makes judgments about all things" because she has "the mind of Christ." Even these journal words are part of the process—this mysterious inner interweaving of observation and reflection and verbalization.

As I lie here in the sun, thinking these thoughts as they come, not trying to be "creative," the wind suddenly gusts and I see a scatter of gold leaves flying down from the maple saplings a few yards away beyond the stream. (In Pensacola, Fall comes in January!) I have been wanting to illustrate my poem ". . . let him hear," about leaves falling from the trees at God's command because they hear and obey him more instantly than we. The image in front of me is perfect. I bring camera to porch, focus, frame, and wait for the wind to blow again and release more leaves for my shutter. My skin tells me when the breeze is beginning, my ears can hear the tinkle of the wind chimes from the porch below. I take shot after shot, and only time and Kodak will tell my success or failure. But the lesson of waiting for the Spirit to move—watching, sensing the "now," obeying the breath, catching him at it—is learned, whether or not a perfect image prints itself on the film.

✳ I'm making some progress on my new project—the sweater I promised to knit for my friend Candace. The pattern is a continental one translated, very badly, from Italian into English, which makes it ambiguous and confusing. The photo of the sweater helps; what sounds impossible in the printed instructions comes clearer when I can see the pictured shape and the patterned textures, knit without seams, all in one piece.

I am feeling, in the roughness of the yarn as the garment grows in my hands, what it is like, also to knit a life. How experimental it is; how the instructions are not always intelligible and often make no sense until I knit them into reality, doing it over and over until it's right and finally something interesting and warm and beautiful takes shape under my fingers. A slow process, stitch added to stitch, row to row, the work picked up and put down at odd moments, the way one adds to one's own life by fits and starts.

Single as I am, widowed after nearly thirty-three years of marriage, I know that I'm knitting a new project, a major one, as big as this long, bulky jacket of Candy's, no incidental sock or collar. For all my wedded years I have knitted traditional Aran fisherman sweaters—complex, certainly, with convoluted cables and ribs and popcorns and honeycombs and trees and mosses and seed stitches, but recognizable within their genre. But this pattern is all new, the style unique. There will be no other sweater just like this, and though I have a pattern of sorts, my own trial and error and decision and will shape it into my own creation.

I am both knitter and knitted one. I can see myself taking shape, all my yarns and fibers looped in rows that hold together and capture within them the tiny pockets of air that insulate and comfort the body—the air is part of the pattern, plained and purled into the pieces. Knitted stitch by stitch, hour by hour, it will take all of the years of my life to finish. *Lord, I hope it looks good when it's done—a seamless garment.*

✻ I'm realizing that I can feel God's presence easily and joyfully in moments of delight. I find him in the light but lose him in the dark. When I'm anxious and reach for him, I can't touch him or sense his reality. That's when he comes in the guise of other people.

Tonight, with some trepidation I auditioned for the West Suburban Choral Union which will perform Bach's St. John Passion in March. The rehearsal (I qualified!) was strenuous, demanding unremitting concentration. My sight-reading skills have lain dormant for too long, but Paul Wiens the director is *good*—knowledgeable, skilled, witty, and a good motivator. The whole evening was exhilarating. It seems miraculous that this marvelous, complex, intense music has leaped the centuries and become a gift in my little life today!

I sat next to Sue Zitzman. It was the first time I'd seen Sue since she moved back to Wheaton following her husband's death in a car accident. We embraced. Such a contact between two widows has special meaning—an almost fierce tenderness that says, "I know. I *know*."

Two

Today we sat—Sue Zitzman and I—and talked and cried and she clasped my hand across the restaurant table among the silverware and dishes, eager to help me face this week with its first anniversary of Harold's death.

Many people have said, "This is your hard week, isn't it? I'll be praying for you." Verses 11–12 of Psalm 139 take on new meaning: "I say, surely the darkness will cover me [overwhelm me] and the light around me turn to night. Yet darkness is not dark to you, and night is as bright as the day. Darkness and light are both alike to you." I feel that even though I can't see him, because often it's so dark, my depression hasn't blocked God out.

But today in church, as we sang "I am the Resurrection and the Life . . . he who believes in me, though he were dead, I will raise him up at the last day," my tears fell freely. *Oh, Harold, you are in another world where I cannot even visualize you—the world of hymns and heaven which seems so remote and abstract. Where is your reality? Why is it so unreal to me?*

✱ The specter of mortality sometimes invades my thinking. Dinner with friends who never seem to age as one sees and knows them from year to year . . . yet not so long ago we were all college students. Youth's slimness, its shiny smoothness grows to flab and wrinkle and crag and the inevitable end. If only I'd known this before H. died. If only I could have told him how much I loved him and would miss him. If only I'd known so that I *could* tell him. If only I could tell him *now*. I can only entrust a message to H. in care of God: "I never knew how much I'd miss you. . . ."

Georgia tells me she dreamed that she and Bernie were dining at our house and after helping me in the kitchen she entered the dining room to see Harold sitting at the head of the table. "Luci thinks she's all alone," he told her, "but I'm watching, and I know everything she does." Another message from God through my friends, and an absolutely supernatural answer to my prayer for Harold to *know* how much I miss him. It means my letter with no address has been delivered by God!

✱ So many letters of awareness. Friends care-full for me that I will not feel pain alone. Prayers from Jim Nyquist, Lars, Eric, Steve, Randy, around my dining room table. I prayed, and broke down completely for what seemed like an interminable interval. I struggled not to sob, to get the words of thanks out beyond the spasm of tongue and mouth and the overflow of eyes—thanks for all Harold had been and had done—for what he'd stood for—anguish in our separation from him. As we rose from the table, Randy put his arm around me and hugged me, then went out and shoveled all my walks clear of two inches of snow that had accumulated during the board meeting.

✱ January 30—St. Mark's at noon. It is so quiet. Yielding to the gusty wind, all the small creaks and groans of the old building sound doubly loud. I am adding silently to the groaning. Karen is kneeling up under the altar lamp. She and I spent an hour earlier this morning together at home as I read aloud through my journal of Harold's last week and cried and trembled and talked and remembered. What relief, after the emotional staleness and flatness, the unreality I had felt all week, trying to capture some real emotion that might tie me to him and the last events he lived just a year ago.

I realize how much I need freshness. How the old hymns, old prayers, old Scriptures sometimes lose reality to me from long exposure and prolonged effort on my part to lend them an immediacy which must often be spurious. I can't even rehash my own old thoughts.

Karen is naturally a mystic, her inner life increasingly alive and searching out new areas of growth all the time. I, on the other hand, am a rationalist, which doesn't quite fill the bill when it poses as a source of spiritual insight. How I want the inner life to bubble up. How I want to hear God's silent voice more clearly, more often, without the apprehension that what I hear is just the working of my own mind.

Just as I wrote these words, our curate came into the sanctuary with bread and wine for Karen and me. We both knelt at the altar and celebrated "Communion under Special Circumstances." One of the passages he read was the Vine and Branches analogy of John 15, with its emphasis on abiding. I had a very distinct mental image of a stunted, withered bunch of grapes on a bunch split off by storm from the main vine. I prayed, in that interval, that I might be closely grafted back onto the vine so that I would once again "bear fruit," and that instead of my striving to abide in him, Christ would bond me to himself. "I *want to be bonded*," was my heart-cry.

✳ Georgia and Bernie picked me up for dinner. At the restaurant we talked about the differences between Harold and me. Georgia recalled his saying to her during his last week, "Poor Lu, she'll always be tormented with questions." He knew, he cared, and though he couldn't change things he never made me feel guilty for my questioning. He knew how much uncertainty and doubt filled me, even though he experienced little of it, about God anyway. Yet the path of clean, steady, absolute faith seems barricaded from me. Is someone else's dream a message for me? ("Lu thinks she's all alone, but I'm watching, and I know everything she does.") I know there are mysteries beyond my experience or comprehension. For Harold, for Georgia and Bernie, the blacks and whites of certainty characterize their faith, while my picture is blurred and indistinct.

✳ Marian brought me an unexpected gift—a tape which I have no memory of recording, of the family gathering two years ago at Christmas, after Harold's lung surgery and before he decided to go through chemotherapy. The tape had faithfully accepted and recorded all the sounds of that winter afternoon. Katy, not quite one year old, was filling the air with shouts and gurgles and the bang of toys. The antique clock was ticking imperturbably in the background. The phone rang twice.

I listened with a thumping heart, both eager and hesitant to hear again the sound of Harold's voice—my first such exposure since his death. But when I did hear it, it seemed utterly natural and characteristic of him, as if he had never left. In the spoken words within the family circle all the issues were being exposed—of life and death, of hope and despair, of love and loss. And the sounds that accompany such realities—sobs, prayers, choked-up voices—made the tape an audible journal entry.

✱ Today the house breathes the incense of floor polish. It is nearly a year since we waxed the wood floors, and I had Kris do it while I was out. The heavy, spicy odor met me at the door when I got back, and all I could think was "Harold ..." He was the one who always waxed and buffed and got such pleasure from our shining floors. To complete the memory of him, I washed the glass of the sliding doors, something else he did with zest. I wondered if he saw me do it and was pleased with their crystal cleanness.

Dropping in at the Mains' later, I noticed on their telephone auto-dial list our names—"Harold and Luci"—along with all their family phone numbers. It's a happy thing to be a part of someone else's family, and a mini-memorial to have his name still listed there, as if we could reach him with a phone call.

✱ A letter quotes the verses from Isaiah about a little child leading the animals, ending with "the earth shall be full of the knowledge of the Lord as the waters cover the sea." It's a verse that has always thrilled me—in a mysterious way. To think of the penetration of the knowledge of God into every nook and cranny of earth in the way the waters fill every submarine crack or finger or whisper of space, is awe-full. It means that all the areas of ambivalence, hostility, ignorance, indifference, will be crowded out and effaced. And that deep, extraordinary knowing will encompass us all.

This kind of promise must be somehow perceived by the very young too. I went to Marlene and Jack's for the evening, with the Boards, and took my new poem about Lauren to read to them. The image is so clear in my head from the Kussros' last visit here, when Lauren recently spent a whole afternoon painting at the breakfast room table, her small head bent in concentration. Her painting of a rainbow is still on my refrigerator door.

How to Paint a Promise in February
for Lauren

Here in my winter breakfast room,
the colors of rainbows are
reduced to eight solid lozenges in a
white metal tray. The child's brush
muddies them to gray in a
glass of water. Even the light breaks down
as it pushes through the rain-streaked
windows, polishing the wooden table
imperfectly.
        Green leaves always turn
brown. Summer died into the dark days
a long time ago; it is hard even to
remember what it was like, stalled
as I am in this narrow slot of time
and daylight.
        Until I look down again,
and see, puddling along the paper,
under a painted orange sun
primitive as the first spoked wheel,
the ribbon of colors flowing out of
my granddaughter's memory—a new
rainbow, arc-ing wet over strokes of grass
green enough to be true.

Three

New York City. Karen and I are in Madeleine's apartment. After stowing our bags, we took a cab to the Cathedral of St. John the Divine—a vast, sprawling complex which we penetrated to Diocesan House and Madeleine's library office. Twenty-foot ceilings, alcoves of old books, dust and must, and four large Irish setters. In one imposing corner is M.'s typewriter and desk, surrounded by icons and carvings and pictures of Hugh and books, and a constantly ringing telephone.

How good to be with her and embrace and talk and drink herbal tea. Madeleine is venting what she calls a "tirage" (emphasis on rage), one of the airlines having lost her suitcase. We both talked about how, in a state of grief, some inconsequential mishap can cause disproportionate anger and emotion. Or, something that moves us emotionally, like music or poetry, brings the overreaction of tears. I told K. and M. I often feel like a loaded, cocked pistol ready for some small finger of feeling to pull the trigger.

In the really fresh, lovely, late afternoon sun we walked the six or eight blocks back to Madeleine's penthouse, with views of gargoyles on the tall old buildings—and the Hudson River gleaming under its skin of river ice. For dinner, Madeleine had cooked a chicken filled with kasha and walnuts in a clay dish, and made a splendid salad with lemon juice, walnut oil, taragon, and garlic.

✳ Karen and I walked literally miles today. The sky was crystal blue and the icy wind bit the cheek.

St. Patrick's Cathedral is magnificent. I saw a perfect photographic angle on it as we approached, with the sun glinting off a glass skyscraper showing between the twin steeples.

In St. Pat's. A time fragment of quiet under the ribbings and high tracings of stone. Hundreds of feet up, the building vaults to a point—reaching for God while enclosing his presence. *You are here, O God, but you are also infinitely high and far away, as is true in my heart sanctuary. I need and want you.*

And I am ready but not ready—ashamed to meet you, shrinking from your righteousness under my human roof of failure. I prayed in the pew next to Karen, together with her, yet each of us reaching separately for God.

✳ Today we walked briskly to the Cathedral of St. John the Divine and enjoyed a tour led by an elderly but vigorous guide who knew well both his Bible and his church history. The newer part of the cathedral is Gothic; the older, Romanesque, with its rounded arches, and dark brown, heavy pillars that seem to say, "Here we are and we're all there is." Gothic, by contrast, reaches up and seems both to adore and beseech in its vertical thrust toward heaven.

Reading "A Walk Through the Cloisters" (where Karen and

I spent yesterday afternoon) I learned more about the contrasts between Romanesque and Gothic architectures and suddenly the link was formed in my mind: The stance of the fundamentalist likens itself in my thinking to the Romanesque—the enclosed barrel vaults, the chocolate brown solidity of massive pillars and ceilinged arches excluding light, the lack of any but rudimentary decoration. It is a monolithic refusal to look beyond itself, particularly above, for light. The Gothic mind, though, admits light and wants more, invites the iridescence of stained glass into its design, the delicate tracery and representation of real and fantastic ornamentation. Flying buttresses allow the support of the building's weight to be transferred outside so that interior space is uninterrupted—no need for heavy pillars. The arches are pointed, like arrowheads penetrating upper space. I see a self-metaphor—I am High Gothic in an often Romanesque sub-culture.

✱ At home again I got the bill from Bronswood cemetery for Harold's grave marker. I feel such relief that it is placed, as if somehow the setting of a metal plate in the ground with his name on it and a record of the span of his life has rescued him from limbo. As I write, the tears are starting, and the tightening of the throat. Why? I know it isn't the essential Harold who is earthed under that sod, but somehow his body is tangible evidence of the reality of his life and presence and person. It is only a skin, like a sloughed-off snakeskin, but it is a precious remnant, a relic.

I worshiped today with some freedom. Rather than demanding that God meet me, be there for me, I felt happy to let him be God, and "freed him" from the bondage of my heart to meet my needs. The first hymn set the scene for me: "Faith believes, nor questions how.... Though the cloud from sight received him ... shall our hearts forget his promise, 'I am with you evermore'?" I was able to sing the alleluias with a pureness of praise unusual for me.

Rick spoke of mountains and clouds. In the Exodus story, God told Moses, "Come up to me on the mountain, and wait there . . . then Moses went up on the mountain and the cloud covered it—the glory of the Lord settled on Mt. Sinai and the cloud covered it six days, and on the seventh day he called to Moses out of the midst of the cloud."

On the heights the cloud obscured Moses' view of everything. He was shut in to God, and he had to wait. This idea of waiting—an open-ended wait to hear from God—mirrors my own assignment. I am accustomed to the sort of immediate, audible, tangible response that occurs between humans when one asks something of another.

For my whole life I have had either a loving father, who wrote home every day when he was away, or a loving husband who made my welfare his concern (as I did his), and who was *available* for me. Perhaps this availability promoted a kind of dependence that slowed my maturity. If I had a problem or a worry or a decision to make, or a success to share—it was so easy to express it to Harold, and to get his response, that I hardly needed God.

Now I am having to grow up. I have been expecting God to be as instantly available as was my husband—to speak to me, to respond in a way that really asked no faith on my part, no waiting, that made no provision for unanswered prayer.

Lent is a time during which, on the high mountain, we wait on God, with human directives and sense stimuli blocked out so that we can listen to and hear him only. As in Psalm 16:7: "I will bless the Lord who gives me counsel; my heart teaches me, night after night."

✱ I'm reading Henri Nouwen's *Genessee Diary*. He admits to not "seeing God all around me . . . always overlooking him who is so close." I haven't put it all together in my mind yet—how I'm to quit the anxious search, yet recognize what's there to be seen. Perhaps the word *faith* holds the answer.

Ideas and concepts that excite me intellectually often attract me more than the realities that lie behind them. My focus is not pure and clear and unselfconscious. My mind distracts me from the vision of my heart.

Another profound perception from Nouwen seems like an arrow to the heart of my desire and failure to believe—that Thomas, though he was skeptical about Jesus' resurrection, "kept faithful to the community of the apostles. In that community the Lord appeared to him and strengthened his faith." Nouwen says: "I find this a very . . . consoling thought. In times of doubt or unbelief, the community can 'carry you along,' so to speak. Thomas's nickname, Didymus, means Twin. All of us are 'two people,' a doubting one and a believing one. We need the support and love of our brothers and sisters to prevent our doubting person from becoming dominant and destroying our capacity for belief."

This throws my relationship to the church into a different and convincing role for me. Rather than viewing my feeling of comfort and "at-homeness" in the Christian community as "using" it, or as a hypocritical or deceptive convenience, I can see it as the church body accommodating and reinforcing its individual parts when they need help, including me. When I have a toothache on the right side of my mouth, the left side takes over the chewing for a while.

I feel this strength of being "carried along" at St. Mark's. Last night I went to the Ash Wednesday service and had the ashes crossed on my forehead and prayed prayers of penitence and entered more fully into my own failure and inadequacy so that, by contrast, Christ's forgiveness meets me in love and redeems my despair. It is the old exchange. And in Communion Christ's mystery and transcendence, his otherness, moves close, becomes available to me.

251

Four

If doubt is a sin, I am a great sinner. I am cursed with questions, damned by doubts.

I wonder whether I have any right, in this state, to teach in a Christian college, minister in church, or write about "adjusting to bereavement" for Christian magazines. Except that my writing has the simple virtue of honesty. I don't want to be a double-dealer, and I am sick to death of the layer of platitudes and petty formulas of evangelicalism. What if the whole subculture of Christianity rises out of an artificial construct? Must I remain faithful to it just because the alternatives are too grim? I am repelled by anarchy, chaos, immorality, amorality, yet much of what seems to be bred in me by pietism is guilt, anxiety, and a nagging spiritual nausea.

I took this to Rick this week, in his office. His response to me: Questioning, probing, is a part of your person. It is your gift to the church. Accept that this is who you are, what you are and stay close within the community of faith.

The thread that seems to hold me to God in this time of flux is Sunday and St. Mark's. When I am in church, things which are heavy with doubt or seem irrational during the week seem possible, believable.

Philip Yancey's article, "Submitting to Freedom," in a recent issue of *Christianity Today* asks: "Is my love for God conditional, like a child's? If things go poorly, do I want to run away or yell, 'I hate you!'?" But I think my struggle with believing God is not so much childish as adolescent—a shifting of values, of tasting independence, a self-centeredness that is too often unaware, careless of the pain it causes in the parent.

I do need to be married to God, to give and receive "the mature, freely given love of a lover." But that kind of love demands maturity, and I realize again my need to grow up.

✳ On my early walk the lip of sun showed above clouds like a small promise. A tender, tentative green is edging along the brown tracings of twigs on the bushes. Knots of buds swell on the trees. After an all-night rain, drops hang from every projection, distilling the subdued light into a pearl-like point of clarity at the heart of each.

A verse I read last night—"He will not let your foot be moved"—is working in my consciousness. Lately, walking around the house in leather-soled shoes on wood floors and my mind on other things, my feet *have* moved, slipped from under me, and several times I've landed in an awkward heap on the floor. But on my morning walk in my Reeboks I have no such trouble. I can stride confidently. I progress in a straight line and my mind can move in a hundred directions as I walk because my footing is secure under me. That's *my* part of the process.

✳ Friday Kris found in the mail her acceptance letter from Western Washington University. Jubilation! Yesterday we mailed her registration fee and her residence hall application. There is finally a sense of sureness to our planning.

✳ Last night we rehearsed the St. John Passion for two hours with orchestra and soloists, but in fragments, so I didn't have a sense of its wholeness. The basses were missing cues and earning Paul Wiens's wrath. It's scary to think of a final performance when we feel so unready. But most of life is like that.

Someone at Chorale practice asked me if I am writing any poetry since Harold's death. My answer: "Of course." Poetry is not detached. It grapples the issues of existence and reality and death through a thousands lenses—the small happenings by which we search out ourselves and God refract the light into colored splinters. I have never lived so intensely or reflectively as during the last two and a half years, and writing is my best way to discover the meaning of it all. It is "Art Translated from Life," the title I have given my Regent course for this summer. When I write poetry I am translating my life into art.

✳ I have been thinking about how the world seems to be divided into a dualism of light and dark. We usually associate God with the light, especially in Jesus, "the light that shines in the darkness and is not overcome by it," "the light that lights everyone who comes into the world." But in his humanity, Jesus himself was no stranger to darkness. When his Father turned the light of his face away, turning from his Son on the Cross, Jesus was left hanging in the deep shadow, crying over the agony of his sense of abandonment. (He must know how I feel.)

And even Jehovah himself, in his mystery, his terrible otherness, has often seemed to his people to be dark. It was Solomon who voiced the realization that "The Lord has said that he would dwell in thick darkness" (2 Chron. 6:1). But out of that enigmatic cloud there flashes from time to time the downward dart of lightning, which will ignite anything in us that is flammable.

Though I am still nagged by doubts, tonight as Carl prayed the prayer of confession with us, I felt as if I were saying to God, *"Here I am, doubt running through me like a seam of coal in the rock. Take me as I am, Lord. I don't know how to be any different. Mine my coal, and burn it. You alone can send the flame that will turn it into heat and light."*

✳ This morning was all foggy and warm. In fog-filtered light I went out with my camera again, still learning my new 500 mm. lens. The air was like silk and pearls—silky and pearly with mist and dew, soft and still so that all the little fringy bushes and branching trees showed clear but grayed; the sun was a gray pearl lying in a nacreous shell of clouds. I found scilla and tulips. The brilliant forsythia is past its prime but still splashes color against the impossibly green grass. Walked along St. Charles to Prince Crossing, then back along North Avenue to where it crosses the DuPage River.

Parallel to the highway I saw the remains of an old bridge—beautiful hand-hewn stone supports each side though the span itself is long gone. An old road must have run along there. The corners and crannies of the bridge and bank are full of white wild apricot flowers. Now the sun is fully out and I can fill my lens with images of water and green and stone and the fragile ice-pink flowers all secluded—a private world lying protected only a few feet below the level of the present highway with its dust and shards of glass and semis and trucks barreling along at sixty-five miles per hour with a withering roar and a blast of wind. It is a summons of sorts, to come back to the old, the persistent, the quiet, the place where flowers shine.

My days are disjointed. The connections are abrupt, never smooth, and all my reactions depend on mood. I plow through distasteful jobs and get them done well enough, but it takes so much energy. I must hoard what little is left for poetry.

✳ Last night I read *The Atlantic* from cover to cover, and there, caught between prose articles on technology and naval strategy, was a poem called "Frog" by Ellen Bryant Voight. (So common a creature to have achieved significance among all the weighty, globe-girdling problems and quasi-solutions.) The poem describes the tensions of Frog, (not just a generic nomenclature but a personal name,) a *she,* who is created for two media but can live only briefly in either without resorting (nice word) to the other. The idea of this ambivalence converted itself in the night, in my subconscious. All the words of the Voight poem fell away, leaving only clear, almost photographic images. The idea of this ambivalence moved metaphorically into the tension of another kind of amphib-ian—a Christian—one who is in this world but not of it, who has tasted the transcendent, whose spirit with its urgent needs lives in an earthbound temporality of eating, working, sleeping, traveling.

The amphibian

Warm after a while on a rock,
drunk with sky, the green
silk, of her skin shrivels
with wind. With a wet, singular
sound, then, she creases
the silver film, turns fluid,
webbed toes accomplishing
the dark dive to water bottom
and the long soak, until her lungs,
spun for air, urge her up

256

to breath.
                    She moves
in two worlds. Caught between
upper and under, she can never
be home. Restless: withering
for wet, and the slope of
her nether ooze, or nostrils
aching to fill with free air
her sodden membranes—
bubble lungs, heart thumping
for life, tympanum throat
pulsing to flood the dark sky
with croaked frog-song.

* Kris and I left the Peugeot in Geneva with a man who specializes in selling used foreign cars to a private clientele. It's rather sad. The car looked deserted as we left it for the last time. I felt as though I'd abandoned my baby at the supermarket where pretty soon they'd start paging the mother. It's a thing, not a person, but it had its own quirkily appealing personality which has tested me over these months. It's like a little death.

I picked up my new Toyota Corolla from the dealer yesterday afternoon. She's lively and tight and shiny. I keep wondering what Harold would think of her. She's one more new thing that he has never seen—one more step forward into the future—one more break with the past.

Five

Today Kris was safely and serenely graduated from high school in a flawless outdoor ceremony under the huge old trees north of Wheaton Christian High. The day was blue and green and gold, perfect for photography, and I wandered around freely with my camera.

Marian, Karl, and children had arrived the evening before, and Jeff joined us later, resplendent in his asymmetrical gray and cream suit bought in Madrid. When Kris received her diploma, I felt as if a major task of my life as a parent had been completed. Somehow, between us, all our kids have moved through high school and beyond. It was good to celebrate. And to hope that Harold was looking on the day with joy. We often laughed at the idea that he would be seventy when his youngest finished high school. But he graduated before she did, from a harder school.

✱ So many thoughts and questions have snagged themselves on a rough corner of my mind this week, only to be blown away in the brisk wind of over-activity. Gone like thistledown. Rick's message this morning—Whitsun, Pentecost Sunday— did lodge with me, though. His thesis: The disciples had no "Plan B" to fall back on if Jesus had not risen, or had proved not to be God in the flesh. It was Jesus or nothing—a weary return to their old life grown flat and stale as dead fish.

For me it is the same. Even if Jesus isn't God, or if God isn't personal, there's nowhere else to go. Perhaps my spiritual malaise, my impasse, derives from my desire to find a watertight, rational proof for the existence of a personal God, which is impossible. But I can focus on the historical Jesus— the enfleshment of the personal God. If Jesus died nearly two thousand years ago, however, what do I have today? The Spirit, who is not geographically or chronologically limited, as Jesus was, but pervasive. Once again, though, I cannot touch, see, hear, smell, *prove* him. I am left with a "person" of the Godhead who at best provides me with a subjective experience. As has always been true, I come closest to having contact with Jesus in Communion—body and blood—physical bread and wine.

✱ I walked this morning for the first time this week. It has been continuously hot, and I have been too sluggish to make the effort. On the home stretch I begin to view our house and land as if through Harold's eyes. What would he think if he saw it now? Pleased? I think so. His little pear tree has grown—pears are actually forming. The lilacs form a high hedge along the bottom of the lot. The square of arbor vitae he planted with such loving care now gives us a place of privacy below the deck, having grown tall and full. The grass slope is nearly weed-free, thanks to regular spraying, and all the tubs and borders are bright with color.

Perhaps he does see all this and feels content. But does he see me, too—my mind a garden with some healthy flowers and fruit, but also weedy patches, still, of ambivalence? Does he wish he could pray and talk with me and encourage me as he used to, giving me a truer perspective?

✱ It's good to be with the Shaws again, all twenty-three of them, on the Cape. Though I'm not a blood relative, I feel loved.

Hands pocketed in my jeans, neck slung with my Nikon, I took a walk up toward the highway and recorded yards of yellow Indian paintbrush and seed pearl grass crowding to the edge of the sandy road. Walked slowly past the cottage of our last vacation here two years back, sounding the draft of my melancholy, feeling it fully, not drawing back, not feeling an obligation to be upbeat, letting loneliness have her way with me. Stared long at the slate-blue shutters, the soft carpet of brown pine needles where we parked the car, where two summers ago Harold had sat in a folding chair in the shade because he'd felt too tired to walk to the beach.

Past the crumpled pink of wild roses, the coreopsis, I wander the empty wooden walkway down to the sand, grasping the handrail he'd held to on both sides for support. Later, out in the car, trying out the feeling of an antique shop where together we'd bought Robin a pair of antique chairs, then to Goose Hummock Marina, past the Lobster Claw (lunch together), and Roberts' (our last anniversary dinner).

It's like thrusting my naked hand deep into the pocket of an old jacket and coming up with lint and a safety pin and half an old theater ticket. A clean pang to be ached through so that next time it won't hurt quite so much.

✱ We are an invasion! Kris and I completed the 2,250-mile drive across country to Bellingham in three and a half days, arriving at Robin's on Monday. All Kris's boxes are now stacked in the basement; Kris herself is in Lindsay's room, living out of duffel bags, and I am sharing a double mattress with Lindsay in the front room, surrounded by suitcases, bags, camera case, etc. It's fairly public. Friends and employees are apt to drop in day or night with a perfunctory knock.

I have seen my new house! Though unfinished, it is lovely — tucked away on its site between the huge Sitka spruce and the whispering, mossy brook running darkly over river gravel and sand, circling half the property. The windows are in, the siding is going up. The proportions look right, the golden unstained pine wood gleaming from its green setting. Robin, Mark, and I have been choosing carpeting, counter tops, siding stain, tile for the woodstove hearth. It is fun to do it all new. But I am still feeling it out, like a cat circling before nestling in to sleep.

Will I really live here? Will I love it? Should I sell the Wheaton house and move? Who would be my friends out here? My church? I find myself praying and trusting God often, deliberately, in my heart, to work things out.

✱ I feel breathless with the rush and fullness of these days at Regent. The classes go too fast; we never have enough time to finish. But I love the spirit of the people. Each one calls for a special kind of love and appreciation. Bonds are beginning to be formed, like the strands of fibrin that hold a blood clot together. Peter, an English teacher came with his family all the way from Sydney, Australia, to take this course before the Fall term at Regent. We have in the group Gerald, a medical doctor, Allen, a playwright/pianist, several teachers, and others, all eager to develop their poetic gifts.

And I'm finding my sense of place — of where I belong. I

have been assigned faculty parking spot #61, office #22, phone extension #331, classroom #1B. I feel wanted here, secure in my office and classroom and in this circle of new friends.

✳ Margaret Smith walked in to class just after we started on Thursday afternoon. Beaming. I wanted to rush over and hug her, but tried to do it with my eyes. It's hard to welcome a soul mate in a crowded classroom with discussion going on. Marg took a seat and fitted in immediately.

The class is cohering. Poems are being forged and cooled and set out for us to admire and chip at. There is a lot of diverse gift, not a dud in the group. It's great fun to watch their delight when their poems begins to dance with a life of their own.

✳ Gordon Fee spoke in Chapel today about *Hesed,* the Hebrew word for steadfast marital fidelity, covenant love, or the word coined by Miles Coverdale—"loving kindness." He read Lamentations 3, and we saw Jeremiah's anguish and distress—called to be a prophet, against his will, with a message he hadn't wanted to give in the first place.

Jeremiah's words bored into me:

> He has besieged and enveloped me with bitterness and tribulation . . . walled me about so that I cannot escape . . . shut out my prayer . . . drove into my heart the arrows of his quiver . . . has made my teeth grind on gravel . . . My soul is bereft of peace. I have forgotten what happiness is, so I say 'Gone is my expectation from the Lord.'

> But this I call to mind and therefore I have hope— the *steadfast love of the Lord never ceases.* His mercies

never come to an end; they are new every morning, great is thy faithfulness.... The Lord is good to those who *wait* for him, to the soul that *seeks* him. It is good that one should *wait* quietly for the salvation of the Lord ... for the Lord will not cast off forever ... though he cause grief, he will have compassion according to the abundance of his steadfast love (*Hesed*).

I carried the promise away with me like a gift.

✻ Today no class was scheduled so that our workshop people could catch their breath and complete their poems and essay assignments. Marg and I ferried out to Vancouver Island.

I hadn't known how thirsty I was for the ocean until we found this beach near Victoria—not really beautiful, but diverse—a stretch of oddities, buttons of wood, mermaids' tears (glass fragments rubbed smooth), stones of worn-down brick. M. and I grab competitively for the treasures. The day has been gently hazy gray—cool, with smudges of rain. Now the sky is blueing, and the sun is coming in and out—an alternate warming and cooling that won't allow you to take anything for granted.

Journaling, dozing, listening to the sea and the sound of wind, there is time to think and feel. This ballad composed itself in my listening mind.

> Oh, my dear has gone—gone away, gone away;
> Oh, my love's gone a long, long way.
> And what do I lack to bring him back?
> Will he come if I kneel and pray?
> Will he come if I kneel and pray?
>
> Oh, my love has left me alone, all alone.

He has left me alone at home.
And what do I lack to bring him back?
Will he come if I grieve and groan?
Will he come if I grieve and groan?

Oh, my love has been gone for a long, long
    time;
Oh, my love's been gone so long.
And what do I lack to bring him back?
Will he come at the sound of my song?
Will he come at the sound of my song?

Oh, my heart's love has gone. Does he never
    hear
My prayers or groans or songs?
If I call my dear, will he draw near?
For him my whole heart longs,
For him my whole heart longs!

My heart's love is both God and Harold. With the song came its melody. I sang it to Marg and we harmonized it together on the beach.

✻ There is the feeling of a completed cycle. Hearing the chorus of "Our God Reigns" sung by the student body, I am catapulted backward three years—to that similar sunny day when Harold had called to tell me of his "walking pneumonia." Now I want to be real before this group, to speak honestly, but without self-pity or sentimentality. I tell them how that day I'd hurried into Chapel late to the rhythm of that song and felt the lift and power and joy of it. I talk about "The God Who Mixes His Metaphors," using the oak tree parable, the poems on "The meaning of oaks" and "All flesh is grass"— emphasizing the paired, opposite values of strength and vulnerability. In a real sense, my speaking here today begins to close this chapter of my life.

✳ Back in Chicago, over dinner with Jim and Carol Plueddemann, I mentioned a call from Madeleine telling how on the one free day she'd had a friend was dying in Boston and she'd been able to be with her during the dying, and later, to preach at her funeral service. M. said she'd been living "in a sense of the absence of God," and this event restored in her a conviction that God *was* actively at work in her life. To Jim, I included myself in the ranks of those who want a clearer, more consistent knowledge of God's present reality, labeling myself "an eternal questioner." On the way home Jim quietly asked me, "Have you been having this problem with doubt for long?" My heart jumped at his courage and sensitivity, his probing of the pathology of my spirit, where most Christians, feeling uncomfortable with unresolved doubt, pacify or pass on to safer, more congenial topics.

I told them how I had found in the writings of many thoughtful Christians an underlying stratum of dark uncertainty, though in our circles doubt is a hard thing to admit; the God-fearing population at large condemns questioners. Yet Jim thinks that, as in George MacDonald's *The Wise Woman,* our tasks and challenges to faith become more difficult the further our journey goes. When I told him I'd relaxed my clutching for God, and am waiting in the dark night of doubt for God to make *his* move (to be, in fact, in control of me), he laughed in relief.

That night I dreamed of Jim. In my dream he seemed to be a persona of Christ coming close and warmly embracing me. I woke at 4:00 A.M. with a sense of buoyancy and relief and light, recalling some of the mind markers on my dim internal journey. The word "Wait" coming to me in the Psalms. From

Psalm 33: "Our soul waits for the Lord—our help and our shield"; from Psalm 71:14 "I shall always wait in patience and shall praise you more and more"—an increase of praise lies ahead. And the challenge of verse 18: "Now that I am old and gray-haired, O God, do not forsake me till I make known your strength to this generation and your power to all who are to come."

And Moses, who waited forty days to see God on Mt. Sinai, and when the waiting was over, the light of the Presence was so strong it even left a residue on Moses' face, so that it glowed as he came down the mountain.

Then Nouwen's words: "Waiting is a period of learning. The longer we wait, the more we hear about him for whom we are waiting."

So I am waiting. And letting go. And have quit striving. I am allowing the community of Christians in the church to carry me along with them. At this moment I feel Jesus coming closer in a subjective but fulfilling way. It is not a rational proof of his reality, but it feels enough for now, as if something is clicking, snapping into place like the buttons on my Lay Readers cassock as I vested this morning to read about Abraham, whose faith, flawed as it was, seamed with doubt, was enough.